## Dedicated to the Women in my Life...

...my mother, Mardell—my first Bible teacher...

...my wife, Becky, who has learned and lived these lessons with me and encouraged me to write about them...

...my daughters, Alyssa, Amanda, and Amber, who are always good sports about being used as sermon illustrations.

# TABLE OF CONTENTS

# CHAPTER ONE
# MY LIFE AS A SADDUCEE

*I* was raised in a church that believed in the miraculous. We never really saw any miracles, mind you, but we believed they were for today. Oh, we'd see prayers get answered sometimes, which was encouraging, but we rarely, if ever, saw the kinds of miracles the Bible described. We'd hear reports about them still taking place in other parts of the world. And when the missionaries came, we'd hear stories of miracles that took place in faraway places.

But at home, we didn't see it. I came to the conclusion that miraculous signs and wonders and healings were needed on the mission field more. It wasn't that they *couldn't* happen at home. We just didn't need it as much. Or something like that.

And we read the stories about Jesus casting out demons and we believed that kind of power was for today, too. Yet, I never met anyone in my church who had ever come face to face with a demonic force. The missionaries had. They would often cast out demons. But we didn't. I came to believe that America was so successfully evangelized that the demons had all left for Africa. I felt sorry for the Africans, but at least they had missionaries who could cast the demons out of them.

I grew up with a very Westernized worldview, a mindset that makes a strong separation between the spiritual and natural.

You might have been raised with the same way of explaining reality. When I was sick, I went to the doctor or the medicine cabinet. I believed in divine healing; I just didn't want to bother God by asking Him for it. He had more important things to deal with, after all. It may sound noble, but it wasn't good for my faith. Modern scientific achievements had given me a Western worldview that had crowded out trusting God for the miraculous. It had crowded out an accurate understanding or appreciation of the spiritual realm.

My scientific, rational, modern mind did not allow me to seek spiritual solutions for physical problems. As far as I was concerned, all mental, psychological and emotional disorders had a scientific explanation. There was a chemical or physiological explanation behind them with a drug to treat them. Or at least a drug to contain them. But nagging me in the back of my mind were a number of unexplained situations that neither medical nor psychiatric science could explain or resolve.

There were those who offered solutions to these nagging thoughts. Any sickness, they said, was a result of sin or a lack of faith. Period. Though I could find a few Scriptures that supported at least part of that thinking, I couldn't find definitive Biblical proof of that idea. Besides, it wasn't particularly encouraging to tell a sick person their illness was their own fault. The condemnation seemed to make them sicker.

But the people with the solutions had even more to say. Some actually suggested that *demons* were behind every sickness and emotional disorder. In my world, all the demons were in Africa. But in their world, demons caused every bad thing. I rejected their fixation on demons, and it wasn't just because of my particular religious upbringing. Common sense conflicted with their explanations, too. I just couldn't accept the stories I heard about people casting out a "spirit of doorknob" or a "demon of chocolate." It was zany things like those that convinced me to have nothing to do with any type of deliverance ministry. Anyone who tried to identify a spirit of doorknob had to be a kook. So I retreated back to my all-the-demons-are-in-Africa doctrine and continued on my merry way, avoiding the questions I had no answer for.

I had become a Sadducee. You have probably heard sermons preached on Pharisees in the church, but I've never heard a sermon on Sadducees in the church. Now a Christian Pharisee, like the Pharisees of Jesus' day, is legalistic, proud, and judgmental. Most of us have been guilty of being a Pharisee at one time or another. I know I have been guilty of it, but my bigger problem was that I was more of a Sadducee than a Pharisee.

The Sadducees are known primarily in the Bible because they didn't believe in an afterlife. I didn't have a problem with that. I knew there was a heaven and a hell. For me, I was guilty of their other major error: Sadducees didn't believe in demons, angels, or other supernatural phenomenon. If you had asked me, I would have said without hesitation that demons and angels exist. But attitudes and actions reveal our true beliefs. Someone can tell me they believe that proper diet and exercise are important, but unless they are eating properly and exercising, I would wonder how seriously they believed that. So it was with me, the Christian Sadducee. I believed in the spirit-world, but lived my life as though everything that happened in the world was only the result of natural, physical, seen forces, and the beings of the spiritual realms just observed without getting involved, or were active on some other continent.

That was my doctrine, and I was like any other Christian who likes to believe that his doctrines are formed completely by his study and understanding of the Bible and by the insights of gifted Bible teachers. But that's a naïve and simplistic thought. In reality, a lot of the great Christian doctrine that came from the pens of the early church fathers was actually a response to heresy. We have great writings of the faith because a church father was correcting error.

Paul and the other writers of the epistles did the same thing. A lot of the Bible was written to correct inaccurate thinking about God, the church, and about what is right and wrong. The same is true for us. We react to ideas that we know are wrong, and that sends us back to the Scripture in search of answers. Another thing that sends us back to the Scriptures is our own personal experiences. When we experience things that are outside of the little belief boxes we set up, we meet a moment of crisis. Will we reject our faith that has no answer for what we have just observed, or will we go back to the Scriptures to see if we missed something?

Without asking for it, I was confronted with one of those unsettling personal experiences, a demonic event in my own home. I wasn't prepared for it; I wasn't looking for it; I didn't like it. Before it happened, I wouldn't have believed it.

My confrontation with a reality outside of my belief box started in the fall of the year, when you send your kids off to school. The first thing they all do is share the viruses they have been storing up over the summer. So my daughter Alyssa, at that time eight years old, came home from school one afternoon looking very pale. She plopped into a chair and didn't move until the nausea overcame her and she began to…well, the thing that nausea produces.

It turned out to be a very intense stomach virus. Without going into too many details, she lost a lot of what was meant to be nutrition, and she became very weak. It was one of the worst stomach illnesses our kids have had. And after the vomiting stopped, the queasiness remained. Sometimes it's hard to know when or what to start eating after being that sick. And that's exactly how she felt. She really didn't know when it was safe to start eating. She became so afraid of throwing up that the fear of sickness began to consume and to control her. We encouraged her to eat something but she insisted she didn't feel like it. At first, we accepted what she said, but eventually we had to conclude that she was well beyond the illness and had to eat something.

Finally, through some "persuasion," we got her to begin eating. A little, anyway. But she wouldn't eat much. She was thin to begin with and couldn't afford to lose weight, but we could see that she was. We encouraged her to eat more. Reluctantly, she complied, but she would never clean her plate, no matter how small the portions were. She would always leave at least one bite, as if to convince herself that she hadn't overeaten.

The fear began to manifest itself in other ways, too. She didn't want to go to school. She didn't want to go to church. She didn't want to go anywhere. She just wanted to stay at home. She had seen a boy vomit at school during the September flu-exchange, and she did *not* want that to happen to her. So it was safer to be at home near her own bathroom. The fear continued to intensify and rob her of her joy. She lost her natural color and looked tired all the time.

We had no idea what we were dealing with, but we knew it wasn't good. We considered taking her to a child psychologist, but the Lord led us to pray about the matter and try some spiritual solutions first. So we had her memorize verses on fear and peace. We didn't tell her why she was learning those particular verses, nor did we draw attention to the fact that they were verses on fear and peace. We simply said it was time she started memorizing Scripture and set up a reward system for her when she learned a verse. So the word of God began to get into her head, and hopefully into her soul.

Then our church declared a "freedom fast"—ten days of fasting for freedom from whatever bondage people were in. During that week of prayer, we began to see a slight improvement, but then strange things began happening with her younger sister, Amanda. She was only five, yet she awoke at about 5:00 a.m. one morning with an intense nightmare. In her nightmare, a large rat with glowing, red eyes (she described it as "Satan's wife") came into our home to terrorize us. My wife, Becky, shared this story with another mom from our church the next morning. This woman had three girls about the age of our kids, and one of her kids also had a dream, about 4:00 a.m. that *same* morning, about *a rat with glowing, red eyes*. I had no psychological, medical, scientific, or Western explanation for what was happening.

Our church had prayer meetings several times a day during the ten-day fast. I chose a day to fast and I went to the meeting after work one evening. I shared with the group that had gathered what had been taking place in our home over the previous three months and what it was doing to our family. They began to pray. They saw visions, they prophesied, we interceded. It was a powerful event.

However, Becky wasn't having such a glorious time at home with the kids. She had asked Alyssa to take a shower and get ready for bed. But apparently, the fear that was preventing her from leaving the house was teaching her to say "no" to just about everything. So, she did something she had never done previously, nor done since. She flat out refused in a demonstrative way. She threw a tantrum of the sort she hadn't done since she was two, when most kids throw them.

While we were praying for her at the church, Alyssa was writhing on the floor and yelling that she didn't want to take a shower. Becky was upset, of course, but also bewildered. Where was this behavior coming from? Meanwhile, at church there was a glorious sense of breakthrough. I came home refreshed and hopeful to a calm house, but flustered wife. We had a "family meeting" where I shared with our kids that the devil was attacking us and that we needed to pray and stand firm.

The next day was a new day. Alyssa was different. And she continued to improve. She began to enjoy school and excel at her studies. By the end of the school year, she looked and acted completely different. Though there were some uprisings of anxiety from time to time, those episodes became fewer and fewer and spaced farther apart until they ended altogether.

I never dreamed that kind of negative, spiritual phenomena could happen to my little Christian family. It rocked my world and put my demons-in-Africa-doctrine on ice. I began to search the word of God for answers. Over the next few years there were other, even more dramatic incidents that happened in my life and in my church. Again, I'd have to go back to the word of God for an explanation.

I determined that my doctrine would be formed by God's word, not by my circumstances, but life circumstances were always forcing me back to the word of God for answers. I went through an important shift. Instead of allowing my beliefs to be influenced by my circumstances, I began to desire to see my circumstances being influenced by my beliefs. Or maybe I should say, instead of allowing my doctrines to be determined by how my prayers were or weren't answered, I began to desire to see my prayers being answered according to Biblical truth.

I began to see things in Scripture about the kingdom of darkness that had never been explained to me before. Putting aside pop theology, I decided to let the word of God speak to me, as if for the first time. I was blown away by what I found, and I finally began to find some explanations for the bizarre things I had observed. That's what this book is about. I take it that you are on a journey also, or you wouldn't be reading it. I invite you to journey with me, as we unlock some of the mystery of spiritual warfare and put more tools in your hands to defeat the lies of Satan in your life and in the lives of the people you influence.

# CHAPTER TWO
# NOT UNAWARE OF SATAN'S SCHEMES

*Oh, my job keeps getting easier*
*As time keeps slippin' away*
*I can imitate the brightest light*
*And make the night look just*
*like day*
*I put some truth in every lie*
*To tickle itchin' ears*
*You know, I'm drawing people*
*just like flies*
*'Cause they like what they hear*
*I'm gaining power by the hour*
*They're falling by the score*
*You know it's getting very*
*simple now*
*'Cause no one believes in*
*me anymore!*

*Oh, heaven's just a state of mind*
*My book reads on your shelf*
*Oh, have you heard that God*
*is dead?*
*I made that one up myself*
*They're dabbling with*
*magic spells*
*To get their fortunes read*
*You know, they heard the truth*
*But turned away*
*And then followed me instead*
*I used to have to sneak around*
*But now they just open*
*their doors*
*No one is watching for my tricks*
*Since no one believes in*
*me anymore!*

"No One Believes in me Anymore"
—by Keith Green[1]

*I*n 2 Corinthians 2:11, Paul told the Corinthians they were not ignorant of the devil's schemes. I'm happy for them. But what about us? Would Paul be able to say the same thing about the church of Jesus Christ today? From my observation, most Christians don't understand much about the devil and his strategies. Doesn't it make sense that if we're going to win the battle against Satan we need to understand what he's up to? Isn't that true of any battle?

It certainly gave Israel a military advantage over the Syrians when God would reveal to Elisha what they were doing (2 Kings 6). It was so obvious to the king of Syria that Israel knew his plans that he assumed one of his officers was a traitor. But his officers told the king that Elisha's prophetic gift enabled him to know what the king was saying in the privacy of his room! We may not need (or want!) to know what Satan is saying in his room, but we do need to have some understanding of the strategies of our enemy. But before we can identify the schemes of an enemy, we first have to know who it is we're fighting against. Even in a friendly competition, it's important to understand the strengths, weaknesses and strategies of the opponent.

When I played high school football, we spent a significant amount of time in each week's "chalk talk" discussing the plays, strategies, and strengths of Friday night's opponent. If the other team had a great running back, we'd assign one defender to watch him specifically. If they had a good quarterback, we'd keep a couple guys back to respect the strength of his arm. We learned everything we could about our opponents and we planned accordingly. Obviously, that's not all we did. We still ran our regular drills and did our calisthenics.

Spiritual warfare is sort of like that. We need to understand Satan's schemes, but understanding them is not the most important thing in spiritual warfare, and knowledge of Satan's strategies alone does not guarantee victory. Spiritual disciplines like prayer, Bible study, Bible memorization, and even tithing are the calisthenics of spiritual warfare that are necessary in the battle against Satan. But just like a football team preparing to play a tough opponent, we must also be aware of whom or what we're up against.

Unfortunately, many—if not most—Christians today are not even aware that we're in a battle. Or, they might think spiritual warfare is optional or just for the spiritually elite, or maybe it's for weird demon-chasers and touchy-feely intercessors and mystical prophetic types. But according to Ephesians 6:12, spiritual warfare is a normal part of the Christian experience and it's not optional. Paul says we are in a fight. He doesn't say just certain of us are in a fight, but all of us. His letter was written to the *saints*[2] in Ephesus, not to the leadership or to the prayer team or the spiritual warfare Sunday school class. He wrote to all of them, and his message is meant for all of us. The message is that we are in a battle.

Every time you are tempted you feel the tension of that fight. Every time you wrestle with your will about stepping out and doing something risky for God, you can sense the struggle. It's a battle. And you're in it whether or not you choose to be. You signed up for it when you decided to follow Christ. Spiritual warfare is not an option for the Christian. It's a necessary and important part of the Christian experience.

One of the reasons we often avoid the topic of spiritual warfare is because we are unaware or unwilling to accept the reality of demons in the world today or the effect they can have on people, even on Christians. James 4:7 tells us to resist the devil and he will flee from us

> God's word tells us to *resist*, not ignore, the devil.

(see also 1 Peter 5:9). It doesn't tell us to *ignore* the devil. That would be like telling someone on a cold day, "Just ignore the cold weather." In Minnesota, where I live, that could be deadly advice. For us to attempt to ignore the devil's deadly schemes, and to suggest to others they do likewise by not "focusing on demons," we aren't doing them any service. In cold weather, we put on scarf, coat, boots, gloves, and hat to protect us from the elements. We aren't focusing on the cold; we're being wise.

In the spiritual realm, we don't ignore Satan; we put on the armor of God and resist Satan's "cold"-hearted attacks. We put on a belt, breastplate, shoes, shield, helmet and sword (Ephesians 6:14-17) to fend off the foul wind of the Enemy. When I step outside my house on a cold, January day, I enter a battle against the elements, whether I want to or not. When we choose to follow Christ, and especially when we choose to step out of our comfort zones to obediently serve Him, we enter a spiritual battlefield, whether we want to or not.

I never used to see that. Whether I was evangelizing, praying, worshiping, or performing other nice Christian duties, the only struggle I recognized was the struggle with motivating myself, or maybe the struggle with other Christians who had a different opinion on how to carry on God's work. My thinking was that Jesus came to love, bless, heal, and save and I should diligently carry on that gracious work.

Then I read 1 John 3:8. It says that Jesus came to destroy the works of the devil. That's funny. I thought He came to die on the cross. And of course, He did. He came to establish a new covenant and usher in God's Kingdom, and His death and resurrection provide the forgiveness and power to enter into and live the Kingdom life. But John describes that advancement as a confrontation with the Enemy. Jesus came, John says, not just to save the world, but to destroy Satan's work. If we aim to carry on His work, we need to recognize that we are not just joining with Him in saving the world; we are joining an army and picking up where Jesus left off in destroying the devil's work. It gives a little different twist to the question, *what would Jesus do?*

## Can Demons Affect Christians?

Growing up as a "Christian Sadducee," I not only came to the conclusion that most demonic activity took place in Africa, I also thought that demonic activity occurred only in those extreme cases when the possessed individual spoke with multiple, ghastly voices, became violent or convulsed. "Normal" people, in my worldview, were not affected by demons and Christians never, ever were. For a Christian person with an uncontrollable, raging temper, or a Christian with an addiction to a sexual sin, or a Christian with suicidal thoughts, I had only a few, unsatisfying explanations. Either they weren't disciplined enough (i.e., they didn't read their Bible and pray enough; basically a works theology), or they had a "disorder" needing psychiatric treatment (e.g., counseling and/or medication), or they had a certain genetic predisposition (e.g., alcoholism running in a family), or they weren't really saved.

The possibility of demons infecting the life of a Christian or controlling certain habits was not an option in my theology. However, the options I did have were not helpful. Try telling a person with a horrible temper who is trying his hardest to control it that he just needs to try harder: "Just read your Bible and pray more." That's bound to make him madder! Tell the suicidal person that he has a "disorder" and you lay upon him the stigma that he's mentally ill. Now he's more depressed. Tell an angry person that his temper was passed down from his dad, his dad's dad, and so on, and you've just sentenced him to a lifetime of frustration. You excuse his immature, irresponsible behavior and teach him to give up. So he says, "It's just the way I am. I can't change it."

Try telling the person addicted to porn that he really isn't a Christian or else he would stop it, and you heap judgment on him. The only place he'll be able to turn to for comfort is his "virtual harem." He loves Jesus—he has just fed his flesh to the point where he no longer is in control of that area of his life. He hates the sin, but he can't stop it. Eventually, he hates himself. So he considers suicide as an escape but then he's told he has a disorder or that he's mentally ill. Now he's depressed, angry, *and* addicted. He begins to agree that perhaps he isn't a Christian after all, or he wouldn't feel and think all those things. Satan is winning that battle, partly because the poor guy doesn't realize he's in a battle! Too often we accept our bondage, thinking that everybody has his own personality quirks, and we agree with the lie that we can't be set free. So we try to learn to live with them and we expect others to get used to the way we are.

How many times have we debated the age-old question, "Can a Christian have a demon?" There are several humorous answers to this question like, "Why would he want one?" Or maybe that isn't so funny. If a Christian really *did* want a demon, couldn't he have one? Of course, no Christian would choose to intentionally invite a demon into his life. But Christians, being human, can choose to sin if they want. That's why it's called "temptation." Sin is *tempting*. If it weren't alluring, we wouldn't have a struggle. So we occasionally blow it. That's why the opening two chapters of 1 John discuss what to do if we do blow it. Christians can sin. And not only can they sin, they can sin repeatedly if they so choose.

As Christians, we are free in Christ to choose to do righteous behavior that leads to life and God's blessings, or we can sin, leading to curses and death. If we allow it, we can make a habit of sin. Repetitious sin is a symptom of an unsanctified area in our lives: a part of us that has not been given over to the Lord. And any part of us that is not surrendered to the Lord is an area that is vulnerable to satanic attack. It's rare to find a Christian who has not been limited at some point in his life by at least one of the more common strongholds like unbelief, fear, pride, unforgiveness, lust, or greed. When we give in to these thoughts and temptations, we sin. And Satan feeds on sin, because whenever we sin, we are agreeing with the devil's plan for our lives. If we agree often enough, that agreement becomes a habit that can control our behavior. When it comes to that, it's more than just an agreement with Satan's ideas; it's more like a contract with his plan. Uncontested habitual sin gives the devil a legal right to an area that was, through thoughts and behaviors, not surrendered to God's control.

Like Francis Frangipane has pointed out, the *habit* becomes a *habitation*[3]—a dwelling where a demonic spirit has been given access to our minds and emotions to manipulate our thinking and behavior. That habitation is what the Bible calls a "stronghold"—a *house made of thoughts.*[4] The Enemy will take up residence in a habitation we have built with our thoughts and behavior. But there are also good strongholds. The Psalmist described the Lord as his stronghold. That's a house built from Godly, Biblical thoughts. But think sinful thoughts often enough, and that thought-habit builds a mental or emotional stronghold—a habitation that a demon can hide in. It's naïve to think that we can deliberately and repeatedly commit the same sin yet remain immune from demonic influence simply because we prayed the sinners' prayer back in '89. Like the famous quote says, "Sow a thought, reap an action. Sow an action, reap a habit. Sow a habit, reap a character. Sow a character, reap a destiny." This quote describes in secular language what we would call a stronghold in Biblical terms.

I didn't believe any of this in my younger days. But then I began to bump into unexplainably out-of-control behavior and freaky mood swings from people who seemed to be sincere Christians. Again, my doctrines had no explanations for the reality I observed. I went back to the Scripture, and I found that the Bible frequently describes bad situations as caused by the Enemy. Along with these explanations, the Word of God contains many warnings about the spiritual forces behind the evil. If the devil cannot affect us, why are we warned about him repeatedly? Why did Paul tell the Ephesians to put on protective armor so the devil's arrows wouldn't hit them (Ephesians 6:12ff)? Why are we told to resist the devil if he isn't a threat (James 4:7)? Why are we told to stand firm if Satan's attacks cannot affect us (Ephesians 6:14)? Why did Peter tell us to be on our guard if the devil can't touch us (1 Peter 5:8-9)?

Clearly, Paul, James, and Peter were all concerned about the safety of Christians because of the devil's schemes, and they warned the church to beware him. We are in a struggle with Satan that Paul compares to a wrestling match. If we don't recognize that Satan is wrestling with us and that we should fight back, we'll find ourselves flat on our back, blinking up at the lights and thinking, "I have a disorder. I'm this way because my dad was this way. It's just the way I am. I missed my devotions today…"

I have found that those who deny the Enemy's ability to affect Christians are those who are the most vulnerable to it. And then they have to find another explanation for their problems—one that fits their theology. That trick never works. Consider these Scriptures that describe the effect of demons on God-fearing people:

📖 **Luke 13:10-16.** Jesus was teaching in a synagogue when he paused to heal a woman who had been crippled for eighteen years. This was an unusual healing, because Luke (a medical doctor) described the woman's condition as satanic bondage. Because the miracle happened on a Sabbath, the religious establishment griped about Jesus working on the Sabbath. Jesus replied, "Should not this woman, a *daughter of Abraham*, whom *Satan has* *kept bound* for eighteen long years, be set free on the Sabbath day from what *bound* her?" (verse 16, italics added). This was not some sinful woman from whom Jesus demanded repentance. Furthermore, her healing/ deliverance was not a dramatic event accompanied by rebuking and shrieking and eyes rolling back into her head. Jesus simply said, "Woman, you are set free from your infirmity" (verse 12). Note this was a "daughter of Abraham"—a woman who showed up for synagogue worship! Neither being a believer nor attending synagogue had protected her from Satan's bondage.

📖 **Luke 22:3** says Satan entered Judas. Think about it. Satan *entered* Judas. And you're thinking, *so what? The guy was a traitor—a fraud.* It's easy for us to think that and only that, since we know the end of the story so well. But think about this from the perspective of one having spent the last three years with Jesus and His disciples. Consider that in Matthew 10:1 Jesus sent out the Twelve (including Judas) to preach, heal, and *cast out demons*. Judas, who at one time had cast demons out of people, was now possessed by the devil. We are not given any indication that Judas did not participate in this deliverance ministry. Though he was a dishonest person, part of him was so loyal to Jesus that he stayed with Him when most others gave up (see John 6:66). Furthermore, I doubt that Judas meant to end Jesus' life with his act of treachery. This seems apparent when, filled with remorse, he returns his blood money and hangs himself.

Why would Judas betray Jesus if he didn't want Him crucified? My opinion is that Judas was hoping that Jesus would have been forced to make a move if He was arrested. I think Judas was hoping to provoke Jesus to some political action by forcing the issue. *Defend yourself, Jesus! Show your power! Kick out the Romans!*

*Oh, and while we're at it, how about I make a buck or two in the process?* But Judas' plan went awry when Jesus cooperated with the betrayal! I think it's possible that Judas was trying to promote God's kingdom with manmade ideas. It was fleshly thinking, and that gave the devil an opportunity to get seriously involved. My point is that I don't see Judas as a demon-possessed non-believer. He was an active believer in Jesus who allowed his greed and fleshly thinking to give place to the devil. The results were disastrous for him.

You might be thinking, "OK, so Satan affected these two at whatever level of belief they were at, but these examples are *before* the cross. The blood of Christ changes everything." And you are right, of course, that Jesus' death and resurrection changes everything. Now we have direct access to God's forgiveness and we have power from the Holy Spirit to live in freedom from sin's power. But there is something that hasn't changed: Satan is still at work, attacking us, so we must be on our guard, walking in the Spirit. If we don't, Satan can capitalize on our lack of faith or our disobedience. Consider the rest of these examples that occurred *after* the cross.

📖 **Acts 5:1-11.** Ananias and his wife, Sapphira, decide to sell a piece of property and give the proceeds to the church. However, it appears that they were doing it just for the recognition since they lied about the size of the gift. They said they brought in all the money, when in fact they held some back. Why did they plan such a thing? What would cause someone to do something like that? Peter's diagnosis was that Satan filled Ananias' heart to cause him to lie to the Holy Spirit (verse 3). The word "filled" in this verse is the same word in Ephesians 5:18, "Be filled with the Spirit." Even in the church, someone can allow his heart to be filled with demonic thought. But was Ananias truly a believer? The context of chapters 4 and 5 say that these events took place *in the church*. And you didn't join the early Jerusalem church unless you were sold out and committed (see Acts 5:13). You didn't just go through a newcomer's class and get a membership transfer from your old church. Because Ananias lied, God struck him dead, and as a result fear seized *the church* (Acts 5:11). Why would the church be seized with fear if some unbelieving liar got struck dead? If that were the case, the church might have been filled with grief, but they wouldn't have been afraid. They might have thought, "You see? That's what we're talking about! God is serious! It's time to repent!" But instead, they were seized with fear because it happened to *one of their own*, caught in a lie, and God judged him. It was a strong statement about how God feels about *believers* who lie to the Holy Spirit. We are not told about any unbelievers, who lie all the time, that were struck dead.

📖 **Acts 8:9-23** tells the story of Simon the sorcerer. When it became dangerous to preach the Gospel in Jerusalem, Philip felt led to leave and preach elsewhere. I think I would have felt led to leave, too. So he arrived in a city in Samaria where Simon lived. Simon was a sorcerer who amazed the locals with his powers. But when Simon heard Philip's message, he believed and was baptized (verse 13).

Speaking as a pastor, I can tell you that Simon was exactly the kind of guy a pastor wants in his church. What a testimony! People around town knew him as a sorcerer, but he had put all that away and was now attending Pastor Phil's church. No need for a high-powered marketing program! Just turn Simon loose and people would come to see how this turn-around could have happened. He was famous, and he most

assuredly had money. A great addition to any fledgling
church! And Simon followed Philip everywhere (verse
13). What pastor wouldn't want that? (Within reason!)
Simon was the type of guy who held onto Philip's every
word, trying to learn as much as he could and apply
it to his life. But he misappropriated his zeal when he
saw Peter and John ministering the Holy Spirit by the
laying on of hands. "Man! I wonder if I could learn to
do that and become a powerful *evangelist*, instead of
a powerful *sorcerer*." So, he suggested to Peter a very
fleshly idea, which was easy for him to do, since he had
lived his whole life that way. "Peter, if I pay you, can
you teach me how to do that?"

And of course Peter, being an encouraging person
said, "Well, actually, Simon, that's not how it works,
but you wouldn't know that since you're new to the
faith." If you know the story, you know that's *not* what
Peter said! He told Simon (paraphrased), "May you and
your money burn in hell because you thought you could
buy the gift of God with it." Imagine if a pastor today
spoke to someone like that! But Peter wasn't done. He
told Simon, "I see what's going on here. Your heart isn't
right. You are full of bitterness and captive to sin." Was
Simon saved? The story is very clear that he believed,
was baptized, and got intensely involved, following
Philip everywhere he went. I doubt Philip would have
baptized him if Simon hadn't renounced his witchcraft
and expressed a desire to follow Christ. If Simon wasn't
a believer, then I wish more churches had "unbelievers"
who were as committed and involved as Simon was!

It's clear that Simon was a baptized believer who
also happened to be full of bitterness and captive to
sin (verse 23). When Simon heard Peter's diagnosis
he requested prayer, an appropriate request for any
Christian in bondage to habits and thought-patterns
from his past. The text does not explicitly say that

Simon's sin was due to demonic influence, but I don't think we're going out on a limb in saying so. Firstly, he was a former *sorcerer*, who would have regularly interacted with demonic powers. Were those powers all gone? It doesn't say. For those that think believing and being baptized should have taken care of that, then why didn't his conversion cleanse him of his bitterness? Despite his newfound salvation, he was still a "captive to sin," something we wouldn't expect of a Christian. Captives are, by definition, in bondage.

📖 **Ephesians 6:10-17.** Paul admonishes the church to put on the armor of God. This example, as well as those remaining, is not a story but a warning to be on the alert against Satan and his schemes. Again, these warnings would not be necessary if Satan couldn't harm us. These verses in Ephesians 6 show that if it were impossible for Satan's arrows to harm us, the armor wouldn't be necessary.

📖 **James 3:14-16** is unique:
> ¹⁴But if you harbor bitter envy and selfish ambition in your hearts, do not boast about it or deny the truth. ¹⁵Such "wisdom" does not come down from heaven but is earthly, unspiritual, of the devil. ¹⁶For where you have envy and selfish ambition, there you find disorder and every evil practice.

The word the NIV translates as "of the devil" in verse 15 is the Greek word *daimoniodes*. It would probably be better translated as "demonic." Somehow, when we see the phrase "of the devil," we have a tendency to depersonalize it. It's a phrase that has been tossed around so much that when most of us hear *of the devil* we think of it as "devilish"—that is, something bad or evil. We tend to forget that the evil thought originated in the mind of an evil being, known as the Devil.

But then, believing in the existence of a person called the Devil is becoming less popular, even amongst Christians. In a 1999 study, George Barna found that 45% of people claiming to be born again don't believe there is a devil.[5] It reminds me of the Keith Green song I opened this chapter with, where the devil says, "It's getting very easy now, since no one believes in me anymore!" In my opinion, *daimoniodes* is better translated as "demonic," which might get our attention in a way that "of the devil" doesn't. James is saying that envy and selfish ambition are not just bad, they are *demonic* in their origin. That is, a demon is behind it. Do you know of any churches, church boards, worship teams, etc, that are plagued with envy and selfish ambition? We might call that a "bad" situation. But according to these verses, churches with these problems are laced with thinking influenced by demons.

📖 **1 Timothy 4:1-3** teaches that some people will abandon the faith and follow "deceiving spirits" and "things taught by demons." The scary thing is that this deception takes place in the context of the church—or what was supposed to be a church. Paul tells Timothy that people in the faith will become so deceived that they will abandon the faith. How does this happen? By listening to "deceiving spirits." Why would someone want to listen to a demon? Obviously, they're being *deceived*, so they don't know it's a demon. They're being discipled by people under demonic influence. (Incidentally, in verse 3 Paul described the doctrines of this teaching as being very legalistic. I'll let you meditate on that one.)

📖 **Ephesians 4:26-27.** Paul tells the church not to give the devil a "foothold." Translated "place" by other versions, this Greek word, *topos*, is where we get words like "topography." It means *opportunity, chance, loophole,* or *opening.* Why is it important not to give the devil a place in our lives? Because if you give him a place—a piece of property—he'll build a stronghold on it. The specific thing Paul was talking about in this verse had to do with anger, but the context also lists dishonesty, theft, crass talk, bitterness, fighting, and slander.

Paul, speaking *to the church,* said that when we give in to those things, we are giving the devil a *place. Topos* was the word used at that time in the shipping industry to describe a port of entry where a ship would pull up to a dock and unload its cargo. It's like Paul is telling the Ephesians, "When you hang on to anger, you're giving Satan a port of entry where he can unload his baggage into your life." Sin is an entry point for Satan to invade our lives. Maybe we don't see it as an invitation to demonic activity, but we certainly give demons permission to manipulate our thinking when we knowingly and intentionally sin and hang onto sinful attitudes. Remember, this warning was written to Christians.

📖 **2 Corinthians 2:10-11.** Paul tells the church that if we don't forgive each other, Satan can outwit us. Satan can outwit *Christians* when they don't forgive.

📖 **1 Thessalonians 2:17-18.** Paul was fully aware of the outwitting ability Satan has. He knew all about Satan's schemes and strategies because he had faced them with pain many times. In these verses, Paul told the church in Thessalonica that he wanted to return to them. He had tried more than once to visit, but *Satan would not let him.*

Imagine that. Paul, the über-apostle—the guy who wrote one-third of the New Testament, planted many churches, took long, dangerous missions trips, expelled demons, healed the sick, and preached fearlessly—this Paul was prevented on multiple occasions from making a trip. The preventer: Satan.

If you were to tell the average American Christian you couldn't make a trip because Satan prevented you, he would tell you that you are "hyper spiritual," or that you give Satan too much credit. But this is *Paul* who said these things. Who is going to tell Paul that he over-spiritualized life events, or that his focus wasn't on Christ? Unless you want to critique Paul's spiritual discernment (and question the inspiration of 1 Thessalonians or the infallibility of Scripture), then we must come to terms with the reality that Satan prevented Paul, multiple times, from making a trip to do ministry. And we think we are immune from Satan's strategies because we prayed the sinners' prayer? If Paul was hindered by the devil, we are arrogant, naïve, perhaps stupid, to think we would never be bothered by Satan's devices.

📖 **2 Corinthians 12:7.** It's not just that Satan can prevent us from doing good things. It's worse than that. In 2 Corinthians 12, Paul describes getting the short end of the stick from a "messenger of Satan" that tormented him. This situation is discussed in more detail in chapter seven, but for now let's suffice it to say that Paul was definitely affected by this satanic attack.

📖 **1 Peter 5:8-9.** Peter warns us that the devil is prowling around, looking for someone to devour. Some think the devil can only look for *unbelievers* to devour. And while the devil also seeks to devour unbelievers, Peter isn't writing to them. He was writing to "God's elect" (1 Peter 1:1). This warning was written to Christians, because Satan is also looking for *Christians* to devour. If we aren't self-controlled, alert, resisting Satan and standing firm in the faith, Satan *will* devour us. If we insist that Satan can't devour a true Christian, then we reduce Peter's warning to an empty threat or manipulative teaching based on a bogus exaggeration.

📖 **Matthew 6:13.** All the above examples illustrate why Jesus taught us in this verse to pray, "Deliver us from the evil one." Again, if the Evil One wasn't a threat, Jesus wouldn't have instructed us to pray against his influence. The above examples show that if not careful, believers can be negatively affected by demonic influences. But the good news is that through Jesus we have protection against the enemy and weapons to do damage to the kingdom of darkness! So my point is not to paint gloom and doom, but to warn us not to be unaware of the devil's schemes (2 Corinthians 2:11). These verses are not meant to strike fear in the hearts of Christians but to impart courage (*en*courage) to *stand up and fight!* Christians most at risk for demonic damage are the ones who won't repent or who ignore that we're in a battle. For the rest of us who believe and take up the armor of God, let's do damage to Satan's kingdom!

## Understanding "Demonization"

So… Do these Scriptures answer the question about whether a Christian can have a demon? Clearly, they teach that demonic forces can have negative effects on Christians if we allow them. If we give the devil a "foothold," we give him a place to set up camp in our lives. That foothold is in the area of the soul—the mind, emotions and will—not the spirit. I'm not talking about demon-possession, because possession has to do with ownership. If we are in Christ, we are owned by God and therefore "possessed" by the Holy Spirit. And because a Christian is owned by God, he cannot be owned by—that is, in the *possession* of—the devil.

I'm not even talking about oppression (whatever that means). It's more than just being harassed. It's a foothold: a place where a demon has attached itself to the soul in order to influence or manipulate thoughts and emotions. It's a stronghold: a habitation where a demon has set up residence by "hiding" behind thought-patterns with the goal of controlling emotions and behavior.

How many times have you heard someone say something like, "I don't know what happened; something just came over me." Maybe something *did* come over them! Now I'm not saying that all these sins are demonically induced and controlled. But I am suggesting that a Christian can have a demonic stronghold whose influence becomes so irresistible that he forfeits control of his behavior in certain areas of his life at times.

Perhaps one of the reasons that the idea that Christians cannot be affected by demons is so common is because of the way English Bibles translate the Greek word *daimonizomai*. Traditionally, English translations have rendered the word as "demon-possessed" or "possessed by a spirit." But the word "possessed" does not actually appear in the Greek. So rather than viewing *daimonizomai* as a demon residing inside someone's body and controlling every crazed facial expression, I think it's more accurate to compare it to a blood-sucking leach. If someone goes swimming and comes out with a leach attached to his skin, we wouldn't say he was possessed by the leach. Rather, the leach has attached itself to him and is sucking his blood.

In the same way, if we "dip" into sin habitually, we open ourselves up for a demon to attach itself to our soul. It's not possession, but we drag that stronghold around with us and it sucks life out of our soul. I'm not saying that every time you sin a demon attaches itself to you. With certain sins and in certain situations, that could be the case. What I *am* saying is that if you tell lies over and over, you are asking for trouble by inviting a spirit of lying to take residence in that area of your mind and will. If you give it control by agreeing with its plan, then it will certainly take the control you give it. Have you ever known someone who compulsively lied to the point where they weren't even aware they were lying? It can be spooky. It might be a lying spirit, and they aren't even aware of it. You want a Biblical example of a lying spirit? Check out the story in 1 Kings 22:23, which is discussed in detail in chapter nine.

Rather than translating *daimonizomai* as demon-possessed, I think it's better translated as "demonized," which can be defined as *being regularly or consistently under the influence or control of a demon to some extent.* That which we have traditionally labeled demon possession has been those cases in which the demon appeared to take over *complete* control of the victim's body, thoughts, and emotions. But the Biblical warnings don't seem to point to that type of obvious demonic control. Rather, they warn us of the subtle, deceptive manipulation that the enemy slinks around doing. It looks like this:

✓ A Christian who simply cannot rid his mind of deadly thoughts like lust, suicide, or violence. He can't keep his mind under control. In other areas of his spiritual life, he's doing OK. So he's not under the total control of a demon, but for whatever reason a demon has significant influence or even control of certain thought-patterns. Paul warned us to "take captive every thought" because we are in a fight to demolish strongholds (2 Corinthians 10:4-5).

✓ Then there's the Christian who is plagued by unreasonable fears that paralyze her, or she has feelings of guilt, sadness, or worthlessness that are completely irrational and destructive. The rest of her life may be impeccable, but those particular emotions are being manipulated by unseen demonic forces, and she beats herself up because she thinks all that thinking originates from her own, unspiritual mind. She's not possessed. She has just given the devil a foothold by listening to the lies over and over.

✓ Or what about the guy who is having unexplained pains in his chest. He's not under that much stress, his heart is healthy, and all the tests the doctors run come up perfect. What's going on? Could it possibly be a demon? Our scientific, Sadduceeical worldview might not think so, but remember that Jesus diagnosed a crippled woman's back as being satanic bondage! In Matthew 9:32, *daimonizomai* is used to describe a man who was unable to speak. When Jesus cast out the demon, the man was able to speak. The demonization clearly had physical impact, as it also did for the man in Matthew 12:22. In that story, the demonized man was both blind and mute. But the Greek does not say that Jesus cast out the demon. Instead, it says He healed (*therapeuo*) the man, a word more commonly used for healing sick and diseased people. Clearly, a demonic spirit affected this man physically, and Jesus' healing power released the man from bondage.

When Jesus came down from the "mount of transfiguration," He delivered a boy from a demon that had baffled his disciples. The boy's father described him as being epileptic. Literally, the Greek word means "moon-struck" because people in ancient times thought that seizures were caused by the moon. In Mark's version of the story, the boy's father immediately identified the problem as a mute spirit that also caused seizures. Mark seems to be describing a grand mal seizure in 9:18. Why would Mark describe an epileptic condition as demonic infestation? Probably because Mark seemed to have great interest in deliverance ministry and the power Jesus had over demons. Early on in Mark (the first chapter) he begins telling stories about Jesus confronting demons, and he talks more about demons than the other Gospel writers do. John, for instance, does not discuss demons at all. The only mention of demons in John's Gospel is when the Jews accused Jesus of being demonized! But Mark had a different emphasis. And in this story, he identified this epileptic condition as being caused by a demon.

I once counseled a young man who suffered from seizures. The seizures began, he said, after his mother died. My sense was that this was not just stress-related but demonically induced, like the boy in Mark 9. So I was not surprised when, during a prayer time with him that a demon manifested, calling itself Epilepsy. After snarling, "I am Epilepsy," the young man launched into full-blown grand mal seizure. But we rebuked the spirit and the seizure stopped. Are all epileptics demonized? I don't think we can say that, especially since Matthew 4:24 draws a distinction between those who were "moon-struck" and those who were demonized. But if a spirit could mess up a woman's back in a synagogue, it would stand to reason that a demon could also be behind some cases of epilepsy.

Now, I'm not suggesting that every lustful notion, or every feeling of fear, or every ache or pain is a demon. I'm just saying that we must leave room for that to be a possibility. To say it could *never* be a demon because we're Christians is to ignore the battle we're in and set ourselves up to be blindsided by an enemy we pretend isn't there.

## Focus versus Aim

Whenever we talk about demonic forces and spiritual warfare, inevitably someone will say, "We shouldn't focus on the enemy—we should focus on Christ." And that is absolutely true. But teaching about demons and spiritual warfare is not focusing on Satan. We need to understand that there's a difference between focus and aim. I *focus* on Jesus. I *aim* at the devil. We *focus* on what we want to see better. We *aim* at what we want to destroy.

> There's a difference between *focus* and *aim*. I *focus* on Jesus. I *aim* at the devil. We *focus* on what we want to see better. We *aim* at what we want to destroy.

For example, when taking a picture, we focus the camera on the object we want to see. (Although everyone's camera now is auto-focus, which doesn't help my illustration!) We don't want a fuzzy picture; we want to see that person or object clearly. But if I'm in a war, I *aim* at the enemy. I don't want his picture. I'm not concerned with the color of his eyes or the style of his hair; I'm only interested in seeing him well enough to get a good shot. I need to make sure it's the enemy and not one of my comrades. What soldier would tell his commanding officer, "Sir, I don't think we should put scopes on our rifles; it puts too much focus on the enemy"? God's word says we're in a battle. Ignoring that information results in disobedience to the Scriptures.

Imagine how ridiculous it would be if I saw a prowler outside your house trying to sneak in your basement window, but I pretend like it isn't happening because I don't want to give the burglar any recognition. When my wife asks me if I'm going to call you or notify the police I say, "No, I don't think we should focus on the burglar. I don't want to frighten the neighbors with news like that. It's kind of a negative approach to life. I'm sure their locks will hold. If I called them, they'd probably think I was saying their house isn't secure. I don't want to be judgmental about the condition of their house." Wouldn't that be weird?

And yet many Christians would say that a warning or discussion about the devil is negative or critical. But being told that a demon is harassing you is no more a judgment about your spiritual life than being warned about a burglar is an indictment on your home's security. In fact, burglars tend to target those houses that appear to have valuables inside. Why wouldn't demons also target people who've got the spiritual "goods"? That certainly was Paul's experience in 2 Corinthians 12. Paul definitely had the goods! Remember, the devil *prowls around*, like a burglar, in order to steal (John 10:10).

I'm from Minnesota. We have lots of mosquitoes here. They feed on people like me—people with blood. Many a picnic, cookout and sporting event have been ruined by the blood-sucking pests. So when we go outside during prime mosquito season, we put on bug spray and stay away from tall grass. No one has ever told me while I was putting on insect repellant, "You're focusing too much on the mosquitoes. Just focus on the picnic." No one has ever told me, as I slapped a biting bug, "You blame every itch on mosquitoes." Instead, they ask, "Did you kill it? Did it get any blood?" Mosquitoes are a great illustration of what demons are to us. We cannot, as Holy Spirit-"possessed" Christians, be possessed by a demon any more than we could be possessed by a mosquito. However, mosquitoes have the ability to bite us and suck out some of our blood *if we let them*. We know what we need to do to prevent it. If we ignore them or don't take precautions, then we suffer the consequences. Though mosquitoes are small, they can carry deadly disease. In the area I live in there is concern about mosquitoes carrying the West Nile virus and encephalitis, both of which can be fatal, and in tropical areas of the world mosquitoes carry malaria, another deadly disease. Small bug, potentially fatal punch.

In the spiritual realm, our relationship to demons is similar. They are pesky nuisances that we need not fear. They are small and insignificant compared to the power available through

Christ, but if we don't take them seriously, terrible things can happen. If we take the proper precautions, we are protected from their attack. But if we ignore them, they have the capacity to do us significant harm.

Our focus should always remain on Jesus. However, as we worship with more intensity, seek God more fervently, study His Word more diligently, we will inevitably provoke retaliation from the Enemy. People have told me, "Before I became a Christian, things were easier. I feel like the devil's attacking me more now. Maybe I should give up."

Right. Like Satan's going to give you a break if you agree with him. Maybe you have felt the same way. It's fairly common. When we grow in Christ, it's like taking ground from Satan—ground he won't give up without a fight.

There are several Scriptural examples that illustrate Satan's reaction to people who focus on Jesus. Whenever Jesus showed up, demons became more noticeable. It's not that they showed up, too, but they were exposed. They could not stay in hiding anymore. They couldn't keep quiet. They couldn't take the holy presence of the Son of God. For example, in Mark 1:21ff, Jesus went to the synagogue to teach. He wasn't looking for trouble or a show; He just wanted to teach. But there was a man in the synagogue that day who was demonized. He probably went to the synagogue regularly, but today Jesus showed up. Without confronting or even singling this man out, the demon began to manifest. "What do you want with us, Jesus of Nazareth? Have you come to destroy us? I know who you are—the Holy One of God!" (I wonder what would happen to some regular churchgoers if we allowed Jesus to show up in our church services? Just a thought.)

This sort of thing happened to Jesus fairly often, and it even happened to Paul as well. In Acts 16:16, Paul was on his way to a prayer meeting, minding his own business, when he was confronted by a demonized girl. The demon couldn't help itself: "These men are servants of the Most High God, who are telling you the way to be saved."

The crazy thing is, the more we experience the presence of God in our lives, the more we will bump into demonic activity. When we press in to know God better, we will often scare up demons without meaning to, without looking for them, and without focusing on them. The presence of God in our lives makes them surface. They can't take it. So while it may appear that we're giving Satan more attention, in reality we are giving *God* more attention. When we do that, either the Enemy fights back or demons freak out and expose themselves.

# CHAPTER THREE
# COMMON MISCONCEPTIONS ABOUT
# SPIRITUAL WARFARE

*A*s we discussed in the last chapter, the most common error in spiritual warfare is the failure to recognize we're in a battle. A similar error is to think that spiritual warfare is only about taming our sinful tendencies. This is the Sadducee syndrome: thinking that demons are not able to influence or affect the lives of Christians. With this error, the presence of demons and their influence in our lives is ignored.

However, once we recognize that demon spirits do exist and they have assignments to tempt and destroy, we must be careful not to over-correct the Sadducee syndrome by blaming *everything* on demons. At this point, you might expect me to say we need to be in "balance." But I'm not talking about balance. I'm talking about *discernment*. Balance would suggest that about half our problems are demonic and half are the struggle we have with the flesh. I don't know what the percentages are, but I suspect it would not be the same for everyone.

Lacking the discernment to recognize the source of the struggle leads to another very common mistake in spiritual warfare: Fighting the wrong enemy. Satan and his cohorts are not the only threat to our spiritual well being. In addition to the demonic personalities Paul tells us about in Ephesians 6:12, we are also warned about the *world* (1 John 2:15-17) and the *flesh* (Galatians 5:16-21). Here's where many Christians who are willing to engage in spiritual warfare make their mistake. Blaming the world, when really it's the devil who is causing problems, means you're fighting an enemy that's not there. And blaming the devil when it's really your flesh cannot result in victory. In order to win a battle against an adversary, you have to engage in the battle *with that adversary*, and not some other of your choosing.

Have you heard the one about the inebriate who was looking for his keys under a street light late one evening? A police officer approached him and asked what he was doing. "Lookin' for muh keys," he mumbled. "Where did you lose them?" the policeman asked. "Oh, I'd say about a block down dat way," he answered. "Why are you looking here?" the officer asked. He replied, "I'm lookin' here because it's too dark to see over there!"

We make the same mistake as the drunken man when we, for example, work harder to discipline our flesh when the actual problem is a demonic attack. And the converse is true. We can make the mistake of blaming and rebuking spirits that aren't there when the problem is that our fleshly desires have not been disciplined. The Bible describes three enemies: the world, the flesh, and the devil. We'll spend considerable time in this book on the devil's schemes, but before continuing the discussion on defeating demonic forces, let's pause to discuss these other two enemies.

**The World**

The New Testament warns us about how evil the world is and that we should not love it. In 1 John 2:15-17, John says,

"Do not love the world or anything in the world. If anyone loves the world, the love of the Father is not in him. For everything in the world...comes not from the Father... The world and its desires pass away." And James speaks even more strongly about it: "Don't you know that friendship with the world is hatred toward God? Anyone who chooses to be a friend of the world becomes an enemy of God" (James 4:4).

What is the world? Before defining it, let's take note of what it isn't. Firstly, John and James are not referring to the Earth. The Earth is the planet God created to do His work with human beings. We have an assignment here. As we shall see, Satan also has an assignment here. His assignment opposes the one God has given us, and so we are engaged in the ultimate (not just epic) battle against evil. The Earth is where this historical drama is played out. The Earth was created by God and God called it good. But it is not our permanent home.

Secondly, "the world" does not refer to the *people* of the world. Otherwise, John would be contradicting himself when he says in everybody's favorite verse, John 3:16, that God so loved *the world*. God loved the people of the world so much that He performed the supreme sacrifice on our behalf. He calls us to love people with similar sacrifice.

What John and James are referring to when they warn us about the world is the *world system*—that is, short-sighted human thinking, corrupted by sin, which is bent on pleasure and only interested in short-term benefits, not eternal consequences. The world system does not see God, heaven, hell, righteousness, holiness, or any other eternal matters clearly. Nor does it want to. The world system pursues entertainment, money, pleasure, and other selfish interests while mocking things of spiritual significance. The world spirit opposes what God wants to do in our lives. It mocks our pursuit of holiness. We are warned against it. It is an enemy.

## The Flesh

1 Thessalonians 5:23 describes the tri-fold makeup of man: spirit, soul and body. There are many excellent discussions on this topic, so I will refrain from rewriting what others have already done such a great job of discussing.[6] For your convenience, however, I'll provide a very brief explanation and how it relates to what the flesh is.

- **✝ Body**: The body is easy to understand. It's our physical makeup with the five senses. It's that part of us that we can see and touch.

- **✞ Spirit**: This is that part of us that is able to communicate with God. We are born into this world spiritually dead (Ephesians 2:1). But when we are born again, our spirits come alive and we are able to communicate with God.

- **♪ Soul**: The soul is not the same as the spirit. The soul encapsulates our personality and is eternal. It will go with our spirit when we die. But here on earth the soul is very much tied to the body and its cravings. The soul is also made up of three parts:
    - **≊ Intellect** (our thinking)
    - **♥ Emotions** (our feelings)
    - **✳ Will** (our decisions)

Some of the decisions the will makes are more intellectual, and some are more emotional. It's typically thought that women tend to make decisions more out of their emotions, and men more out of their intellect, but this isn't necessarily the case. Guys like to think that they bought that new car because it had front wheel drive, great gas mileage, and a superior crash rating. But if they're really honest about it, they'll admit they bought it because it's fast, and it's red. That's an emotional, not intellectual, decision. Most of the decisions we make are some sort of blend of what we know in our minds (our connection to the facts) and what we feel in our hearts (our connection to our desires).

The body is that part of us that connects us to the physical world around us. The spirit is that part of us that can connect us to God. But the soul is that part of us that connects the body to the spirit. The soul is the "command central" for our being, which is why Satan spends so much energy targeting our souls. If he can get us to believe a lie (in our intellect), he can get us to feel something negative (in our emotions), and we'll be inclined to make poor choices (with our will). That's why so much has been written in the last few years on the battleground of the mind. It truly is where the battle is won or lost. If I believe the truth (intellect), I will feel (emotions) and behave (the will) accordingly. If I believe a lie, my emotions and behavior will bear that out. Most of the issues of bondage discussed in this book are in the area of the soul.

So what is the flesh? It's unfortunate that we don't really have an adequate English word that equates to the Greek word *sarx*. Poorly translated words are the cause of a lot of misinterpreted Bible passages. But in some cases, like this one, the translator doesn't have a lot to work with, due to a lack of words to choose from in the target language.

A Mexican pastor I knew well told me about a Spanish-speaking pastor that was trying to preach in English. In Spanish, the word for "flesh" is *carne*, which is also the Spanish word for "meat." So the poor guy, trying to preach in English about the flesh, kept telling the congregation to beware of the "meat." But some of our English Bibles don't do much better when they translate flesh as "sinful nature" or "human nature."

The NIV and NLT, for example, translate *sarx* as "sinful nature" (see Galatians 5:16ff) and the TEV (Good News Bible) uses the phrase "human nature." All of these translations are misleading. It's clear that Paul is defining the flesh as an enemy in these verses, so we'd think we'd be okay calling the flesh the "sinful nature." But 1 John 4:2-3 says Jesus appeared in the flesh (*sarx*), so to suggest that the flesh is the "sinful nature" is to suggest that Jesus had a sinful nature. I suppose one could argue that Jesus had a sinful nature but never yielded to that nature. One could say that, but I don't know why one would! Jesus lived a sinless life, and though tempted, we aren't given any indication that He had any nasty cravings for sin that troubled Him. He was tempted, yes, but there's no indication that He struggled with desires that annoy or even torment people.

What about translating *sarx* as "human nature"? This is maybe slightly better, but it's still confusing. Exactly what is the human nature? In Galatians 5:19-21, it sounds like the human nature (if that's what the flesh is) is bent toward evil. Again, Jesus had a human nature, since He was fully human, yet He was not bent toward evil like the rest of the human race.

Maybe it would help to go back to the beginning. When God created Adam, He declared all of His creation, including Adam, as *good*. Human nature, as it existed at that time, was good, not sinful. When Adam sinned, human nature became *corrupted*. We are sons of Adam who have inherited his tendency toward sin. Our human nature, like that of our ancestor Adam, is not evil, but it has been corrupted. Therefore, it desires evil things.

More literal translations (e.g., KJV, NKJV, NRSV, NASB and ESV) translate *sarx* as "flesh." This is the most accurate term, but there still remains a problem: What does "flesh" mean? There are many great definitions out there that are very difficult to remember and describe. And if the translation that says "flesh" doesn't provide a definition, the reader's interpretation is up for grabs.

I find it helpful to define the flesh to be simply the combination of the body and soul. In the original creation, the flesh (body and soul) were uncorrupted and truly good. When we sin, we corrupt the flesh and give way to Satan's perversion of what God created good. The body is good. So is the soul: the mind, emotions, and the ability to make decisions. We need all those things to serve God. But

> The "flesh" is the desires of the soul and body.

once we get into a sin pattern, our flesh begins to crave all sorts of ungodly things that aren't good for us. This is what Paul was talking about in Galatians 5:16-17. The flesh wants what the spirit hates, and vice versa. They are opposed to each other. Incidentally, I think the CEV has done something interesting with the Galatians 5:16 passage: "If you are guided by the Spirit, you won't obey your selfish desires." *The Message* does something similar by translating flesh as "compulsions of selfishness." Of course, these are not literal. But they don't use a potentially confusing term like flesh, nor do they cast an incorrect doctrinal slant by defining *sarx* as something evil. However, "selfish desires" or "compulsions" aren't perfect, either. Modern English just doesn't have a word to completely capture the concept.

So the flesh describes the natural and normal desires and cravings of our humanity that have been corrupted by sin. And though originally good in God's creation, our flesh is now selfishly bent toward behaviors that satisfy those corrupted longings; behaviors the Bible calls sin. Therefore, the flesh is another enemy to the work of God in our lives.

Demons aren't the only enemy of our faith. Our flesh is a major contributor to spiritual dysfunction. This is where we must be astute and discerning about what enemy we are facing. If we have a weakness in our flesh, but blame a demon for it, we are shadowboxing; fighting an enemy that isn't there. On the other hand, if we're being harassed by an evil spirit but blame it on our own evil desires, we live in frustration. "Why do I feel this way and think those nasty thoughts right in the middle of my devotions! What's wrong with me?" There may not be anything "wrong" with you; you may be the target of demonic harassment. James tells us to submit to God and *resist the devil* (James 4:7). If the devil is the culprit, then we resist *him*, not the flesh. It's critical to know what we're fighting.

There were several times when studying in my office of the church I pastored in western Minnesota when I would hear an unusual knocking coming from the church foyer area. It was loud enough that it could not be ignored. It took me a while to figure it out, because the culprits that would congregate in front of the glass doors would scatter before I got there to discover who they were and what they were doing.

They were crows. (And you thought I was going to say they were demons, didn't you?) As near as I can tell, they saw their reflection in the glass door and attacked, thinking it was a rival crow. They picked a fight with an enemy that wasn't there. In fact, the enemy was their own reflection! In the same way, we can make the mistake of attacking what we think is a demon, but it's just our undisciplined flesh staring at us. Ouch. So, on the one hand we can make the mistake of rebuking demons that aren't there, and at other times we might blame ourselves for struggles that are induced by demonic forces.

So how do we know whether we're fighting demons or it's just our flesh? Answering this question depends on the situation and requires discernment and the leading of the Holy Spirit, but I'll pass on to you a rule of thumb that can be helpful. In her book, *Intimate Friendship with God*, Joy Dawson suggests that if you are facing a "normal" temptation for you—a struggle that you commonly face or a natural desire that you have—it's probably the flesh. Our flesh perceives the object of the temptation to be a good (that is, *desirable*) thing.

The problem with sin is not that it's so bad; it's so *"good!"* That's why we feel tempted! It's something desirable that looks, feels and tastes good to our flesh. Eve perceived that the fruit would be beneficial for her intellect and yummy for her taste buds. So she ate it. That's why we sin, too. We think there will be either short-term or long-term benefits of that decision.

On the other hand, Joy Dawson suggests that if you are tempted to do something totally out of character for you, something outside the realm of your typical struggles, then that may be a demonic temptation. For example, I know many emotionally healthy people that have had suicidal or heinously violent thoughts skip through their minds. Maybe you have, too, at one point or another.

I once heard a pastor share that he had a fleeting thought of homosexual experimentation, though he was completely straight and had never desired anything of the sort. The temptation popped into his head right after he had finished a counseling session with a homosexual man. Temptations like these are almost certainly demonic in their origin. Remember, Satan tempted Jesus with things that were not part of His usual desires. For example, I'm certain Jesus never struggled with the urge to worship Satan, yet the devil tempted the Lord with just that idea. Clearly, that was a demonic temptation and not a struggle with the flesh. And Jesus dealt with it accordingly. Jesus battled the Enemy, but at the same time He was also training His flesh (through fasting) to be obedient. Hebrews 5:8 says that Jesus learned obedience through suffering. If Jesus had to learn obedience, how much more do we! And if we are tempted the same way Jesus was, as Hebrews 4:15 says, then we must be aware that demons will "speak" to us as the devil spoke to Jesus.

Demons have the capacity to suggest thoughts to our minds, but it's widely accepted that demons cannot read our minds. The Bible doesn't say anything on this one way or the other, with the possible exception that only God is omniscient. Whether one needs to be omniscient or not to read thoughts may be debatable, but it would appear from practice that Satan is not able to read our thoughts. If it appears that he can, for example the success of mind readers, it's all smoke and mirrors. That is, a demon whispers the same thought to the mind reader and to the one whose mind he is reading. So the thought that was "read" was actually planted by a demon spirit who clued the mind reader about what was going on. It would then stand to reason that a mind reader would only be able to read the mind of someone who was spiritually weak or susceptible enough to receive a message from a demon without knowing where it came from.

But how many times do we receive messages from demons and aren't aware of it? If we're tempted the same way Jesus was, and Jesus was tempted by hearing input from the devil, then we have, too, and we probably weren't aware of it. What happens is that a demonic spirit will drop a thought into our minds in the first person. "I wish I were dead," it will whisper. We "hear" that thought in our head, think it comes from us, when really we have no desire to be dead whatsoever. But there it was, bouncing around in our brain, so it must have come from our thoughts, right? Not necessarily so! We need to be discerning about what is our weak flesh speaking foolishly and what is an attack of a demonic spirit. If you tell it to be silent and leave, and then the thoughts go away, well, there's your answer.

Discipline the flesh; resist the devil. Both are needed for spiritual growth and victory. Get them confused, or underestimate their influence, or deny the existence of the devil, and you will be frustrated in your spiritual growth.

## The Devil did not make you do it

Even worse than fighting the wrong enemy is the error of blaming demons for every difficulty or temptation. In reality, my flesh has been corrupted enough that I am capable of sinning without Satan's assistance, and your flesh is probably just as capable. Let's not give the devil that much credit! Francis Frangipane believes in the existence of a demon he calls "Wrong Focus" whose assignment is to get Christians to believe that all problems are caused by demons.[7] (It's interesting that he would blame such thinking on a demon. Think about *that* for a bit.)

Although I don't know of a way to prove or disprove such a statement, I would agree with him that many Christians do have their focus twisted into a paranoia about demons that gets their eyes off Christ. Sometimes *we* (our flesh) are our own worst enemy. And the flesh doesn't need to be rebuked, it needs to be trained and disciplined. But training and discipline isn't exciting. It's not particularly glamorous and doesn't sell like demon bashing does. People would rather watch high-powered TV evangelists casting out demons from the safety of their living rooms than listen to their pastor tell them that spiritual disciplines like fasting and tithing (see Malachi 3:8-9) promote power and freedom in your life. It's not glamorous or exciting, but it's true. And it's the truth that sets people free (John 8:32).

## Chapter Four
## Satan—Who is he and Why is he Here?

Since it's important to understand the devil's schemes, it stands to reason we should start by understanding who the devil is. When my football team scouted opponents, we knew the names and even weights of many of the guys we'd have to tackle. We tried to understand them so we would know how to defeat them.

In the spiritual realm, we need to know who Satan is if we're going to understand his weaknesses and how we can defeat him. This is not as important, of course, as knowing Christ and His power over Satan. But Paul makes it clear that we should not be ignorant of Satan's tactics (2 Corinthians 2:11). On the following pages, I'm going to share with you a doctrine about Satan that I admit may seem unconventional. But every idea is built completely from Scripture.

I, like you might have been, was raised in a Bible-believing, evangelical church that rarely talked about demons and rarely taught about Satan. What I was taught about Satan is what you were probably taught, that Satan was originally named Lucifer and that he led a rebellion in heaven and was kicked out, taking one third of the heavenly host to serve him as demons. That's what I believed and understood as I grew up and I even taught as much after I entered the ministry as a second career.

It was while preparing a sermon on this topic that my thinking was challenged. I planned to preach on rejection, and was working on the idea that Satan wants people to feel rejected because *he* was rejected—*ejected* from heaven—and he wants everyone else to feel the frustration of what he felt. So I grabbed my concordance to look up the key Scriptures that teach about Lucifer's rebellion to make my point. But I couldn't find "Lucifer" in my NIV concordance.

*Oh well*, I thought, *this concordance probably isn't exhaustive.* So I did a search on my computer for "Lucifer" in the NIV and came up with nothing. Hmm. So I grabbed my grandpa's trusty *Strong's Concordance* and found the entry for Lucifer. But to my surprise, I found only one reference. I was thinking there had to be at least two or three. It seemed odd to me that we had developed such a detailed account of a rebellion based on just one verse. Some have even developed the doctrine to the detail of suggesting that Lucifer was the most beautiful angel in heaven and that he was in charge of worship. Some have also facetiously added that when he was kicked out of heaven he landed in the orchestra pit, which is why there is so much controversy over what music to sing in church!

So, I looked up this one lone verse in the NIV, and to my surprise I discovered—as if I was reading it for the first time— that had I not been fed the doctrine of Lucifer all my growing up years with the King James Version, I wouldn't have seen it in there. The reason my NIV search had not yielded any hits on Lucifer is because it doesn't occur in the NIV—anywhere. What the KJV calls "Lucifer," the NIV calls "morning star."

That's when I began to look at the texts on Satan as if for the first time, and what I discovered has given me a whole new insight and confidence in spiritual warfare. It has also given me a better understanding of the nature and purpose of God which has motivated me to participate in spiritual warfare with a clearer sense of direction. I now want to take you through the texts we have traditionally used to support the Lucifer rebellion. I would ask you to consider them with an open mind. Read them in your Bible. Allow the Lord to speak to you through His word, not through your fourth-grade Sunday school teacher who was simply reciting popular thought from her Sunday school quarterly. As we work through these Scriptures, I will share with you what I believe is the true origin of Satan, and why it's important for us to know this.

There is a point to this. This is not just some interesting discussion to provoke your thinking. There's a point to this that should impact how we view God, evil, temptation, spiritual warfare, sanctification—just about everything that's important in the Christian faith.

Ready? Fasten your seatbelt. We're about to take an exit off the freeway of tradition. But I believe this road, though less traveled, is one of truth.

### Isaiah 14:12-20. "The morning star has fallen."

This is without a doubt the most popular verse supporting the Lucifer rebellion, since the KJV says, "How art thou fallen from heaven, O Lucifer, son of the morning! How art thou cut down to the ground, which didst weaken the nations!" Sounds like a pretty strong argument for the Lucifer rebellion story! Or is it? We'll take a closer look. To do so, we'll look at this verse from three different angles: First, what does the word "Lucifer" mean? Second, who does Lucifer appear to be in the context of Isaiah 14? And third, are there any historical or cultural clues that would help explain who Lucifer is?

### 1. Who is Lucifer?

We get the name or word "Lucifer" from the King James Bible. Other translations, like the NIV, translate "Lucifer, son of the morning" as "morning star." What's the deal with that? That's pretty different! The Hebrew word translated "Lucifer" or "morning star" is *heylel*. Most scholars believe it means "light-bearer" or "shining one," a noun based on the verb *halal* which means "to shine."[8] Other scholars, however, say *heylel* is a form of the verb *yalal*, meaning "to howl."[9] Still other scholars believe *Heylel* was the name of the Babylonian king in Isaiah 14, or maybe a title for him.

Of these three possibilities, none of them resembles the name "Lucifer." The word *lucifer* is actually a Latin word for "light-bearer." It comes from two Latin words: *lux* (light) and *ferous* (bearing). In the early fifth century, a man named Jerome translated the Bible into Latin—a translation known as the Vulgate. It was a special translation for Christians since it was the first translation directly from Hebrew and not from the Greek Old Testament, called the Septuagint.[10] So it was Jerome who first used *lucifer*—"light-bearer"—to translate the Hebrew word *heylel*. But he didn't invent the word. Lucifer was a Latin name for the planet Venus, the third brightest object in the sky after the sun and moon. Shortly after sunset, Venus appears as the "evening star." But when it appears shortly before dawn as the "morning star," it was called Lucifer.

> "Lucifer" was the Latin name for the planet Venus when it appears before dawn as the "morning star."

Why would Jerome use a Latin name for Venus to translate *heylel*? It would appear that Jerome was influenced by the Greek Septuagint. Since the Septuagint is the Old Testament written in the language of the New Testament, it's a connection between the Hebrew Old Testament and the Greek New Testament. It gives us another perspective on how people interpreted the Hebrew Scriptures around the time Jesus walked the earth. The Septuagint translates Isaiah 14:12 as follows:

"How did you fall from heaven, *Heosphoros*—
you who rise in the morning?"

(Author's translation)

*Heosphoros* was a Greek god known as the *morning star*. The word literally meant "dawn-bringer." In other words, *Heosphoros* is the Greek version of *Lucifer*, what we know as Venus.[11] Getting confused? Maybe a picture would help:

### Isaiah 14:12

|  | Hebrew Scriptures | Greek Septuagint | Latin Vulgate | KJV |
|---|---|---|---|---|
| **Word used** | *heylel* | *heosphoros* | *lucifer* | Lucifer |
| **English translation** | "light-bearer" | "dawn-bringer" | "light-bearer" | Venus |
| **English equivalent** | *(that's what we're trying to figure out)* | Venus | Venus | Venus |

To answer the question, "Where did Lucifer come from?" we have to follow a meandering trail of bizarre choices of the translators. You can follow that trail in the above chart from left to right. Isaiah, written about 690 B.C, used the word *heylel*. The Septuagint, translated about 100 B.C., translated *heylel* as *heosphoros*. Actually, they didn't just translate *heylel*, they interpreted *heylel* to mean the planet (or god) Venus. Then Jerome, in about 382 A.D., translated *heosphoros* as *Lucifer*. The translators of the KJV should have been translating from the Hebrew Old Testament, but they were already biased because of English Bibles that already existed. In fact, the King James Authorized Version of the Bible was actually a revision of the Bishops Bible, produced in 1568. Check out Isaiah 14:12 in the Bishops Bible:

> Howe art thou fallen from heauen O Lucifer, thou faire mornyng chylde? Howe hast thou gotten a fall euen to the grounde, which didst weaken the nations?

But the Lucifer tradition in English Bibles didn't even start there. If we go back another 200 years, to the first complete English Bible, translated by John Wycliffe's colleagues, we find this in Isaiah 14:12…

> A! Lucifer, that risidist eerli, hou feldist thou doun fro heuene; thou that woundist folkis, feldist doun togidere in to erthe.

That's what English (actually, Middle English) looked like in 1384. We can't read it very well, but we can definitely see that a precedent was set by retaining Jerome's Latin word, *Lucifer*, in this verse. Why did they retain Lucifer? And why did they use Lucfier and not Venus? Since people in ancient times did not know that Lucifer, the "morning star," and Venus, the "evening star," were the same planet, a reference to the morning star would be associated with Lucifer, not Venus. The earliest we can find that the second planet from the sun was called Venus was in 1290, less than 100 years before Wycliffe's Bible was translated.

Furthermore, Venus was the name of the Roman goddess of love and beauty, especially sensual love. The Latin word *venus* referred to love, sexual desire, or beauty (hence the word "venereal"). Had Wycliffe's colleagues changed Jerome's "Lucifer" to "Venus," it would have cast a different slant on the text. So it's possible that the mention of Venus to a reader of that era would have prompted thoughts of mythology, not astronomy.

There is an interesting thing about the planet Venus that sets it apart from other planets that are visible to the naked eye. Shortly after sundown Venus, the "evening star," appears low in the sky. Though it is brighter than the other stars and planets, it doesn't rise as high or last long into the night. Then, if you get up before sunrise you can see Venus again as the "morning star" (called "Lucifer" before astronomers knew it was the same planet). In the early morning, Venus reappears low in the sky for a short stint before it disappears in the overwhelming rays of the sun.

For her fourteenth birthday, I bought a telescope for my daughter, Amanda. The first time she sighted in on Venus, she called me to come quickly to see it before it disappeared. With the telescope's magnification, I watched Venus move downward in the scope as it quickly set in the western sky. Sort of sounds like, "How thou art fallen from heaven" a bit, doesn't it? The astrological behavior of Venus might have influenced the translators of the Septuagint to render *heylel*, "light-bearer," as Venus, a symbol of something or someone we're trying to figure out.

Perhaps the biggest challenge with understanding *heylel* is that there are no other occurrences in the Old Testament of that word. So if "morning star" is the correct translation, then it's the only morning star in the Old Testament. However, the New Testament talks about a "morning star" that can give us some clues. A morning star is mentioned in Revelation 2:28

but not clearly identified. It's safe to say, though, that it isn't Satan, since the "one who overcomes" (verse 26) will be given this morning star. Then in Revelation 22:16 Jesus says, "I am the Root and the Offspring of David—the bright star of the early morning" (author's translation). Very clearly Jesus calls Himself the Morning Star.

Another even more interesting reference is in 2 Peter 1:19 where the morning star is said to rise in our hearts. In this verse, Peter used the Greek word *phosphoros*, not the phrase "bright star of the early morning" that Revelation uses. If you check out our little table of Isaiah 14:12, you'll see a similar Greek word, *heosphoros*. It turns out that *Phosphoros* was another name for *Heosphoros*. *Heosphoros* meant "light-bearer;" *Phosphoros* meant "light-bringer." Both were names for the planet we call Venus, but was also known as Lucifer in Latin, depending on the time of day. This is where it gets really interesting. When Jerome translated the Latin Vulgate, he chose the word *lucifer* to translate *phosphoros* in 2 Peter 1:19. Though there is only one occurrence of the word Lucifer in the King James Bible (Isaiah 14:12), there are *two* occurrences of Lucifer in the Latin Vulgate. The other is in 2 Peter 1:19. So it's time for another picture:

### 2 Peter 1:19

|  | Greek New Testament | Latin Vulgate | KJV | NIV |
|---|---|---|---|---|
| **Words used** | *phosphoros* | *lucifer* | day star | morning star |
| **English translation** | "light-bringer" | "light-bearer" |  |  |
| **English equivalent** | Venus | Venus |  |  |
| **Meaning** | Jesus | Jesus | Jesus | Jesus |

In this verse in the Latin Bible, Peter tells us we ought to look forward to "lucifer" rising in our hearts. What? How can Lucifer be *Satan* in Isaiah 14:12 but Lucifer is *Jesus* in 2 Peter 1:19? In my opinion, it's unfortunate that the early translators of the English Bible decided to use the Vulgate's *lucifer* instead of translating the Hebrew *heylel*. It fueled the whole Lucifer rebellion story, and created an inconsistency with 2 Peter 1:19.

About a hundred years or so before Jerome inserted *lucifer* into Biblical traditions, the creative theologian Origen (A.D. 185–254) proposed that the "light-bearer" of Isaiah was actually Satan. Tertullian, who lived about the same time as Origen, took it a step farther and posited that Satan's role in heaven was that of the leading angel. Perhaps they borrowed from a tradition that can be vaguely traced to the book of 2 Enoch,[12] which tells the brief story of "Satanail" rejecting the Lord and then going down to the earth (2 Enoch 18:3). What is the book of 2 Enoch, you ask? It's a book that is part of the pseudepigrapha, a collection of writings mostly between the Testaments that are attributed to various prophets and Biblical characters, though they are not accepted in the canon of either the Hebrew or Christian Bible. Despite their non-inspired status, these books did influence early Christian thinking to some extent, and it's possible that the creative juices of Origen and Tertullian were inspired by this writing. So when Jerome translated the Latin Vulgate and assigned the name Lucifer to Isaiah's light-bearer, the stage was set for Origen's doctrine to get popular.

As we have seen, the earliest English translations of the Bible retained Jerome's use of *lucifer* instead of translating the Hebrew *heylel*. The King James Version (1611) kept the name

> In the third century A.D., a theologian named Origen proposed that Isaiah's light-bearer was actually Satan.

(or title) Lucifer alive and the success, popularity and influence of the KJV made Lucifer a fixture in the English language. In 1667, fifty-six years after the KJV Bible was published, John Milton wrote *Paradise Lost*, using Lucifer as a name for Satan. Other poets did the same thing and the idea grew in popularity. Curiously, the New King James Version, despite its usual accuracy—especially its Old Testament translation—retained Lucifer in the Isaiah passage. These decisions by translators, poets, and theologians alike have not only kept the doctrine alive, but made it so popular it is considered common knowledge and practically part of the basic tenets of the Christian faith.

But let's go back to Origen, the guy who got the idea rolling. Do you really want to embrace Origen's creative doctrines about Satan? Most Christians have accepted Origen's theory of the origin of Satan (sorry, I couldn't resist that play on words). But most Christians reject Origen's doctrine about the *end* of Satan. Origen believed that in the end, Satan would be saved.[13] I'm not sure what he did with Matthew 25:41 where Jesus spoke of "eternal fire prepared for the devil and his angels," or how he interpreted Revelation 20:10 that says the devil "will be tormented day and night for ever and ever" in "the lake of burning sulfur."[14]

We all grew up being taught that Lucifer was Satan's name before he fell from heaven. We haven't known it any other way. But we have to realize that in the history of Christian doctrine, this has not always been taught. Prior to Origen and Jerome's time, the name Lucifer was not connected with Satan or anything evil. It was connected to Jesus, as 2 Peter 1:19 does, and it was considered so favorable amongst Christians that it was a common name for parents to name their sons! Thus we have in Christian history the likes of Lucifer of Calaris, who did a lot of writing on the Trinitarian debate. His followers were called "Luciferians."[15] They were *not* Satan-worshipers!

The million dollar question is: How could Satan be the "morning star, *son* of the morning" in the Old Testament when Jesus is *the* Son, the Morning Star of Revelation? Did Jesus take over that post vacated

> How could Satan be the "morning star" in Isaiah when Jesus is the Morning Star of Revelation?

by Satan or is there something else going on? One argument says that Satan, originally Lucifer, once was the bright morning star but lost that rank because of his rebellion. His position was then given to Jesus. This argument leans on examples where Jesus and Satan are both called something similar. For example, they are both referred to as "lions." But it's a weak argument, in my opinion. Jesus is *the* Lion of Judah, whereas Satan prowls around *like* a roaring lion (1 Peter 5:8).

As we shall see below, the context of Isaiah 14:12 is a prophecy about the king of Babylon. If there is another, hidden meaning, it must be proven, not assumed. Insisting that the morning star of this verse is Lucifer, now known as Satan, is really hard to prove in light of the whole Bible, especially when Jesus is referred to as Lucifer, the morning star, in the New Testament.

## 2. What does the context tell us?

Since this verse is the only occurrence of *heylel* in the Old Testament, we'll have to examine the context carefully to determine who or what *heylel* is. Isaiah 14:12 is part of a prophecy about Babylon that begins in chapter 13. At this point, you might do well to set this book aside for a bit and pick up your Bible and read the book of Isaiah—at least the first 14 chapters. In Isaiah, you'll find the writings and stories of a prophet in the midst of a nation on the decline. Isaiah prophesies multiple times about the sins of the people of Judah. He also foretells the coming of the Messiah in prophetic language that New Testament writers like Matthew help to unpack and sort out for us. Primarily, Isaiah's message was one of warning regarding the sins of both the nations of Israel and Judah. The nation of Israel eventually fell and was taken into captivity during the time of Isaiah's ministry.

He also prophesied about other sinful nations at that time. These prophesies begin in chapter 13 with a prophecy about Babylon, continue with Moab in chapter 15, then Damascus in chapter 17, Cush in chapter 18, Egypt in chapter 19, more on Cush and Egypt in chapter 20, back to Babylon in chapter 21, and finally back to Jerusalem in chapter 22 before moving on to Tyre in chapter 23. You get the idea. That's the context of chapter 14, a two-chapter prophecy regarding the sinful nation of Babylon. Let's take a closer look at it.

The prophecy begins in Isaiah 13:1 by identifying this message as an "oracle concerning Babylon" that Isaiah saw. The opening verses describe armies from faraway lands coming to do destruction to Babylon. Great fear is predicted. In typical, apocalyptic style of the prophetic writings, Isaiah describes the "day of the Lord" with language that was probably figurative: The stars of heaven going dark, the sun darkened, the moon snuffed out, and the world punished for evil.

Now while it's possible that these pictures literally describe what the end of the world will look like, it's more probable that these words are imagery (strong figures of speech) to describe a dramatic end to the nation of Babylon. This type of language was common in prophetic literature to describe significant events. For example, Ezekiel's prediction of Pharaoh's demise included the stars being darkened and the moon's light being extinguished (Ezekiel 32:1-8). In Acts 2:14-21, Peter quotes Joel's prophecy on the Day of Pentecost as being fulfilled, including the sun being turned to darkness and the moon to blood. We can take these cataclysmic references as being word pictures and not literal, astrological events. This doesn't undermine the credibility of Scripture or suggest that the Bible isn't literal. The *meaning* is literal, though idioms and word pictures cannot be taken literally in a word-for-word sense. This is simply a peculiarity of human languages. It makes language more interesting. We do the same thing ourselves. How often do we describe some (minor) crisis as "the end of the world"? Is it literally the end of the world? No. But that's not what those words mean! It means something awful happened. That's what the prophets often did when they used similar word pictures.

Not all the language in the prophecy is coded with word pictures. Some things are clearly identified. In Isaiah 13:17, the Medes are named as the ones behind the warring destruction in the preceding verses. And in verse 19, Isaiah says God will overthrow Babylon as he did Sodom and Gomorrah. The devastation will be so great that Babylon will not be inhabited again. Instead, jackals and hyenas will move in. That dramatic prediction brings us to the end of chapter 13.

Chapter 14 begins with a word of compassion for God's people. Though they weren't part of defeating Babylon, they will have opportunity to taunt them (verse 4). The taunt will be about how peace has come now that Babylon has been destroyed. It is in the middle of this taunt that we get to our key verses, 12 to 20.

> [12]How you have fallen from heaven, O morning star, son of the dawn! You have been cast down to the earth, you who once laid low the nations! [13]You said in your heart, "I will ascend to heaven; I will raise my throne above the stars of God; I will sit enthroned on the mount of assembly, on the utmost heights of the sacred mountain. [14]I will ascend above the tops of the

clouds; I will make myself like the Most High."
[15]But you are brought down to the grave, to
the depths of the pit. [16]Those who see you
stare at you, they ponder your fate: "Is this the
man who shook the earth and made kingdoms
tremble, [17]the man who made the world a
desert, who overthrew its cities and would not
let his captives go home?" [18]All the kings of the
nations lie in state, each in his own tomb. [19]But
you are cast out of your tomb like a rejected
branch; you are covered with the slain, with
those pierced by the sword, those who descend
to the stones of the pit. Like a corpse trampled
underfoot, [20]you will not join them in burial, for
you have destroyed your land and killed your
people. The offspring of the wicked will never
be mentioned again.

"How you have fallen from heaven, O morning star, son
of the dawn!" (verse 12a, NIV). Before we hastily identify this
as a reference to Satan, former resident of heaven, we must
remember that we're in the middle of a prophecy about *Babylon*.
If this prophecy is a reference to something other than Babylon,
it must be clearly shown. A different interpretation—like the
Lucifer rebellion—should not, and cannot, be assumed.

To be convinced of it, we must be able to answer the
following questions: *What in this verse suggests that Isaiah is
talking about Satan? And that Satan fell from heaven? How
do we know Satan was in heaven in the first place?* Nothing in
this chapter says, "Satan started out in heaven as a good angel
and went by the name Lucifer." Satan is not clearly identified
in Isaiah 14. If there is a double meaning in this prophecy, the
trick to the second meaning is cracking the code of Isaiah's
figures of speech.

However, Isaiah's figures of speech do not seem to fit

our traditional understanding of Lucifer. Verse 12 says, "You have been cast down to the earth, you who once laid low the nations!" Notice the order of events in this verse: You once laid low the nations, but now you have been cast down to the earth. But there *were* no nations when Lucifer was allegedly cast down. There were no *people*, as Satan was already present in the Garden of Eden prior to the birth of Cain.[16] A more likely explanation of the phrase is that it was *Babylon* who once laid low the nations, but had now been cast down to the earth; that is, cast down to the ground.

### 3. What does history have to say?

Verse 13 says, "You said in your heart, 'I will ascend to heaven.'" If Lucifer/Satan was already *in* heaven, why would he need to ascend *to* heaven? The phrase in Verse 14, "I will make myself like the Most High," is almost universally accepted as Lucifer's ambition. But why? How do we get that out of these verses? Doesn't it make just as much sense to say that it was the Babylonian king that wanted to exalt himself to the position of God? Certainly the chief sin of man from day one has been to make himself his own god. Again, before we look for a second meaning to "morning star," we must first look at the original meaning of the word, which was certainly meant for the king of Babylon.

Understanding a little bit about Babylonian culture, politics and religious orientation is helpful. Some scholars believe *heylel* was a title or proper name for the king.[17] Other experts think when Isaiah called the king of Babylon *heylel* that he was taunting the king. Still other researchers point out that Babylonian kings liked to place themselves on the level of the gods, and with Babylon's strong connection to astrology it's easy to see how the king would be referred to as "Venus" or some other star.

Furthermore, some theologians believe that these verses don't describe Satan boasting about being like God but are the boast of the Babylonian king against Babylon's pagan gods. Where do they get this from? Firstly, the word from which *heylel* comes from was often used in mythology. For example, the sun being a shining thing would be considered a goddess to the pagans. Referring to the king with the language of mythology suggests he saw himself as a god.

Secondly, there was a Canaanite myth about a god—the dawn star—who attempted to scale the heights of heaven but was ever condemned to be cast down into Hades.[18] So it's possible that the Babylonian king would have known exactly what Isaiah was referring to when Isaiah accused him of wanting to ascend to the mountain of the gods but would be cast down. The king would have known that the prophet was comparing him to the defunct Canaanite god.

Thirdly, verse 13 says he boasted that he would sit on the "sacred mountain" (NIV) or "the mount of the congregation, in the sides of the north" (KJV). Traditionally, we have assumed this to be heaven. But *north* in Hebrew is *Zaphon*, a name well known in the Ugaritic[19] language as the mountain of the *gods*. *Zaphon* is *not* where the God of Israel is enthroned. He's in heaven itself.

So the verse sounds like a boast of a pagan king that he would exalt his throne above his gods or above the mountain where he believed the gods assembled. The "assembly" or "congregation" is actually a reference to pagan gods. You might not be convinced that this is the right interpretation of the text. But the weight of evidence is much stronger for this argument than a Lucifer rebellion.

In verse 18, the Babylonian king is taunted by being compared to other kings of the world: "All the kings of the nations lie in state, each in his own tomb." Other kings all lie in state in their tombs, but Babylon's king is cast out of his tomb without a decent burial (verses 19 and 20). Again, one could try to suggest that this is figurative language about Satan. Or, you could just say this is literal language about the king of Babylon. The book of Daniel describes how the Jews were in Babylon when, in 539 BC, the Persians overthrew King Belshazzar and took over Babylon.[20] There was a Babylonian rebellion in 482 BC, but King Xerxes put down that rebellion and destroyed it. Though Babylon was later rebuilt, the Seleucids captured it in 312 BC, when it fell into disrepair.[21] No more Babylon.

At this point I should probably address the question of whether the reference to Babylon itself is a figure of speech. Is Isaiah 14:12 talking about the literal nation of Babylon, or is it figuratively speaking of Satan's evil kingdom? The context of the chapters surrounding Isaiah 14 suggests the literal nation of Babylon, and the historical witness described above confirms that. But there is certainly a figurative Babylon that the Bible also speaks about in 1 Peter 5:13 and six times in Revelation. For the sake of argument, let's look at the possibility of Isaiah 14 talking about the demise of a figurative Babylon—Satan's domain. The Revelation passages have a message similar to Isaiah's:

Revelation 14:8, 18:2..... Babylon the Great is fallen!

Revelation 16:19........... God poured out His wrath on Babylon.

Revelation 17:5.............. The prostitute drunk with the blood of the saints had this inscription on her forehead: "Mystery, Babylon the Great."

Revelation 18:10........... "Judgment on Babylon came in one hour," lament the kings of the earth who had committed adultery with her.

Revelation 18:21........... An angel predicts that the great
city of Babylon will be thrown
down never to be found again.

All these verses seem to point to future events. In fact, not just events in the future but the *last* events of the future. Chapter 19 of Revelation begins a worship celebration rejoicing about the overthrow of evil. I think it's safe to say that the Babylon of Revelation is a figurative Babylon, since the literal nation of Babylon basically ceased to exist in 312 BC.[22]

Some people believe that the Babylon described in Revelation 17 is actually a reference to Rome, especially when verse nine describes seven hills, which matches Rome's terrain. So while Revelation and Isaiah may be talking about different Babylons, their descriptions about what happened to their Babylons are similar. They are not describing a *setback* for Babylon, but the *destruction*—the *end*—of Babylon. If Isaiah's Babylon is figuratively Satan's kingdom, then it cannot be a look back to Lucifer's fall from heaven; it must be a look forward, like Revelation's Babylon, because it describes destruction. And Satan's kingdom has not been completely destroyed yet. That's where you and I come in. As we promote the Kingdom of God, we destroy Satan's kingdom. That's why I wrote this book and why, I hope, you're reading it.

<u>So is there a hidden mening?</u>

If Satan isn't the morning star of Isaiah, how could the king of Babylon be the morning star? Good question. As mentioned earlier, calling the king the morning star may have been a taunt. But we must admit that prophetic language uses imagery and metaphors that are difficult to decipher, especially when it's 2,700 years and several cultures away. It would be a bit presumptuous to assume a complete understanding of all these word pictures. However, I would like to suggest an interpretation that makes more sense—given the whole counsel of Scripture—than the Lucifer-Satan interpretation. Ready for this?

If there is a secondary meaning to these verses, could that figurative person—the morning star of Isaiah 14:12—be a reference to Adam? After all, it was Adam who fell. We don't need a prophetic metaphor to know that. It's explained clearly in Genesis. He fell from grace and fellowship with God. He lost intimacy with God and was forced from the Garden. It was Adam who was enticed to follow the Serpent's advice to make a stab at becoming like God (Genesis 3:5) in terms of knowledge. The crime of exalting oneself to be like God is the accusation of Isaiah 14:14. Adam was guilty of that. But was he the "morning star"? Consider this: The New Testament refers to Adam as the "first man" (*adam* is the Hebrew word for "man") and Jesus as the "last man" or "last Adam" (see 1 Corinthians 15:45). Luke, in his genealogy of Christ, refers to Adam as the son of God (Luke 3:38) and of course Jesus is called, throughout the New Testament, the "only begotten" Son of God. If Jesus, the Son of God and Last Man, is the Morning Star, then wouldn't it make sense that Adam, the son of God and First Man, was also a morning star?

You may not be convinced yet, but there's more data to look at. Let's leave Isaiah for a bit and move on to the very popular Ezekiel passage. I'd suggest that you read Genesis 3, Isaiah 13 and 14, and Revelation 22 very carefully before you cry "heresy!" In the meantime, let's stir the pot some more!

> Could the morning star be Adam? After all, it was Adam who fell.

**Ezekiel 28:12-19. "You were in Eden, a guardian cherub."**

This reference is not to *heylel*, the target of Isaiah's prophecy. This prophecy is directed to the ruler of Tyre. Again, as with the Isaiah passage, if these verses are a figurative reference to someone or something other than the king of Tyre, it must be clearly shown. We should not *assume* these verses are talking about Lucifer.

Ezekiel, like Isaiah and most of the prophetic books, contains many warnings for God's people and other nations who were living sinfully. And as with Isaiah, the context of Ezekiel's passage is a series of prophecies for other nations. Chapter 25 contains prophecies about Ammon, Moab, Edom, and Philistia. The prophecy and lament for Tyre begins in chapter 26 and continues through 28, before Ezekiel moves on to blast Sidon at the end of chapter 28 and Egypt in 29. Let's take the verses of chapter 28 apart and see if Ezekiel was hinting toward a second meaning and if so, what that second meaning might be.

Verse 2a: "In the pride of your heart you say, 'I am a god.'" Again, we have traditionally believed that this was a reference to Satan before his fall. But there's nothing in this text that identifies Satan or that he had a positive role in heaven. As with the Isaiah passage, we must first recognize the original meaning was about Tyre's king. And in his arrogance, the king declared himself to be a god, no different from what all the Pharaohs did and what Herod did in Acts 12:22. If we are looking for a second meaning here, it makes more sense to again look to Adam, who vied via shortcut to be like God.

Verse 2b: "But you are a man and not a god." Hmm. I have a hard time seeing this applying to Satan, who is clearly not a man. But the king of Tyre was. Oh, by the way, Adam was a man, too.

Verse 5 describes how this person amassed great wealth

through his skill in trading and the result was a proud heart. So that doesn't sound like *either* Satan or Adam. Obviously, this is a reference to Tyre's king.

Verses 6 through 8 describe God's attitude and response toward this person's pride. God plans to bring foreigners and ruthless nations against him. Verse 7 says swords will be drawn against his beauty, wisdom and shining splendor. Many would use this verse to say how beautiful Lucifer was (however, Satan's "beauty" still exists in deceptive form, masquerading as an angel of light as 2 Corinthians 11:14 says), but I say they are reading *into* the text, not reading what's there. Tyre was a beautiful, shining kingdom that had become proud and exalted itself, and now God was bringing it down.

Verses 9 and 10 predict the death of the king. If this applies to Satan, exactly how does one *kill* him? Clearly, this part of the passage could only be a reference to the king.

A lament for the king of Tyre then begins in verse 12. Ezekiel was instructed to say this *to the king of Tyre*.

> [12]"You were the signet of perfection, full of wisdom and perfect in beauty. [13]You were in Eden, the garden of God; every precious stone was your covering, sardius, topaz, and diamond, beryl, onyx, and jasper, sapphire, emerald, and carbuncle; and crafted in gold were your settings and your engravings. On the day that you were created they were prepared. [14]You were an anointed guardian cherub. I placed you; you were on the holy mountain of God; in the midst of the stones of fire you walked. [15]You were blameless in your ways from the day you were created, till unrighteousness was found in you. [16]In the abundance of your trade you were filled with violence in your midst,

and you sinned; so I cast you as a profane thing from the mountain of God, and I destroyed you, O guardian cherub, from the midst of the stones of fire. [17]Your heart was proud because of your beauty; you corrupted your wisdom for the sake of your splendor. I cast you to the ground; I exposed you before kings, to feast their eyes on you. [18]By the multitude of your iniquities, in the unrighteousness of your trade you profaned your sanctuaries; so I brought fire out from your midst; it consumed you, and I turned you to ashes on the earth in the sight of all who saw you. [19]All who know you among the peoples are appalled at you; you have come to a dreadful end and shall be no more forever.'"

—ESV

Obviously, there is figurative speech in this quote. The king of Tyre was never in Eden, and certainly was not a "cherub" in the classical understanding of that word. Furthermore, we know that all have sinned, so he could never have been blameless, as verse 15 states. So this is either figurative language about how far the king of Tyre fell, or Ezekiel is talking about someone else. The traditional view says this is a description of the fall of Lucifer. I'm going to suggest, as you might have gathered, that if there's a figurative interpretation to be accepted, then Ezekiel was speaking figuratively of Adam and the fall of man. Let's take a closer look.

Verse 12b: "You were the signet of perfection, full of wisdom and perfect in beauty." Where does the Bible say that Satan was ever perfect? Only here, I guess, except Satan isn't explicitly identified. However, we know that Adam was created and placed in the Garden in a sinless state—perfect, wise, and beautiful.

Verse 13: "You were in Eden." Clearly, Satan had a presence

in the Garden through the serpent, but there also were two others in the Garden: Adam and Eve. We have always assumed that this was a reference to Satan, but I challenge you to read it again, as if for the first time, and ask yourself if the message sounds more like Adam than Satan.

Verse 14: "You were an anointed guardian cherub." The interpretation of this verse hinges on what a cherub is. Our English word cherub comes from the Hebrew, *kerub* (not to be confused with the chocolate chip alternative). The Bible's first introduction to these creatures is when Adam and Eve were put out of the Garden of Eden and *cherubim* (plural of *cherub*) were placed with flaming swords to guard the entrance and to prevent the first couple from returning to their original homestead (Genesis 3:24). The word cherub occurs ninety-one times in the Old Testament, and one third of these, thirty-one are found in Ezekiel. Throughout the Old Testament, cherubim were described in various ways, sometimes having four wings, other times six wings. They could have four faces or one. Often they would have the face and hands of a human. There were carved cherubim in the Temple, and the presence of the Lord was often described as dwelling "between the cherubim."

Of all the occurrences of this word, these two verses in Ezekiel 28 seem to stand out as odd. Normally, cherubim were amazing creatures of worship accompanying God's presence. But in this case, they are identified with some sort of failure. Was this describing a heavenly host that botched its celestial job, or was this word used figuratively for a human being? Perhaps a clue is the description of *guardian* cherub. Is the word "guardian" meant to describe Adam, who was given the job as caretaker of the Garden (Genesis 2:15)? That certainly fits the description of a guardian, a job from which Adam fell. You may think that's stretching the text a bit. I say that's less of a stretch than jumping to the conclusion that this prophecy about the king of Tyre is actually a coded message about the fall of Satan from his original job in heaven.

Verse 15: "You were blameless in your ways from the day you were created, till unrighteousness was found in you." We can easily see Adam in this verse. But can we see Lucifer? For this I look to the words of Jesus who described Satan as the father of lies who was a murderer from the beginning (John 8:44). It doesn't sound like Satan ever had any goodness about him, but that he was vile from the very beginning. (I know, you're thinking now, "So did God create Satan evil? Did God create evil?" Hang in there; I'll get to that one, but taking that one on now would distract us from Ezekiel.)

Verse 16: "…you sinned; so I cast you as a profane thing from the mountain of God, and I destroyed you."[23] We have assumed that this was Lucifer being expelled from heaven, an event we have no clear description of in the Bible. However, we have a very detailed account of the expelling of Adam from the Garden.

Verse 17 contains the most compelling argument for these verses being a reference to Satan. "I cast you to the ground." The NIV says, "I threw you to the earth." Where was this person before being thrown to the earth? We assume heaven. But couldn't this also be a figurative reference to being thrown down in general? That is, thrown down to the *ground*, as the ESV says? Or, cast back to the dust from which he came? As it turns out, the word that the NIV translates as "earth" in this verse has a wide range of meaning. It can be translated as *land, country* and yes, *ground*. If the secondary meaning of these verses is a description of Adam's fall, we can easily understand that Adam's sin introduced a brand new concept—death—the inevitable return of the physical body to the earth.

Whatever figure of speech Ezekiel was pointing to, verse 17 marks a shift. He uses language that seems to fit only the king of

Tyre and no one else: "Your widespread" and "dishonest trade" (verses 16 and 18, NIV); being a "spectacle...before kings" (vs 17); and "you have come to a horrible end and will be no more." This all sounds like judgment specifically on Tyre.

So as with the passage from Isaiah, when this passage is put back into its original, intended purpose and read at face value, it's extremely difficult to seriously spin a tale about Lucifer being ejected from heaven. The Lucifer story is often supported by using one passage to interpret another, but that breaks a basic rule of Bible interpretation. It's sort of like looking up a definition in a dictionary and the definition uses a word you don't know. So you look up the new word and its definition uses the original word you looked up! It's circular logic, creating codependent interpretations that, like any codependency, are ultimately dysfunctional.

# CHAPTER FIVE
# SATAN'S JOB PHASED OUT OF HEAVEN

*I*n the previous chapter, we looked at the two most common texts used to support the theory of Lucifer's rebellion. In this chapter, we will look at two other well-known texts, and then move on to some other passages that are less known. We will explore a different explanation for Satan's ejection from heaven other than the Lucifer rebellion, and consider why this understanding is so important.

## Luke 10:18. "Satan fell from heaven."

We now move on to what is probably the third most popular text used to build the doctrine that Satan was ejected from heaven. Luke 10:18 says, "[Jesus] replied, 'I saw Satan fall like lightning from heaven.'"

Before jumping to conclusions, the reader should be aware that the word "heaven" in the verse does not necessarily mean the dwelling place of God. This Greek word (*ouranos*) was also used to refer to the sky. Considering that Satan is the "prince of the power of the air" (Ephesians 2:2), it's possible that Jesus was saying that He saw Satan fall from the "sky." With this understanding, we might paraphrase Jesus' words with a metaphor of our own: "Satan got shot down."

More interpretive help can be found in the context of the verse. Chapter 10 of Luke begins with Jesus sending out seventy-two other disciples to go ahead of him. He gave them detailed instructions about how to minister and how to behave in each town. He sent them out and they returned in verse 17. They reported that even the demons submitted to them in Jesus' Name. Jesus' response to this report was verse 18, quoted above. He then went on to explain that He had given them authority to trample on snakes and scorpions (probably referring to demons) and to overcome all the power of the enemy.

The context of verse 18 seems to fit with *current events*, not historical events. The disciples came back and said, "Jesus, it was great! When we used your Name, the demons did what we told them!" And Jesus responded with, "I know, it was awesome! You gave Satan a black eye. I saw him crumble and fall from heaven."

That interpretation seems to fit the context better than the traditional approach that suggests that Jesus' attitude in verse 18 was more like, "Yeah, you guys did great. You really socked it to Satan. It reminds me of the time, way back before man was created, when I saw Satan falling out of heaven." I think when we leave this text alone—in the context it belongs—we don't see Lucifer being ejected from heaven before the dawn of time. Instead, we see the disciples of Jesus doing serious damage to the kingdom of darkness. The damage was so great that Satan fell like lightning from his place of power in the heavenlies.

**Revelation 12:7-12. War in heaven. Satan cast down.**

There are at least three main ways to view this text. The traditional view says that this passage describes Lucifer's rebellion and excommunication from the host of heaven. This view is completely dependent on the interpretations of Isaiah 14 and Ezekiel 28 referring to Satan's eviction from heaven. In my opinion, those verses don't provide an adequate foundation for the Lucifer story, which ought to prompt us to look for other possibilities in the Revelations 12 passage. So another view suggests that Satan hasn't been hurled down yet, but that this will happen at some point in the future. Still another view sees these events coinciding with Jesus' death on the cross.

This text is my personal favorite, because it begins to unfold the mystery and the purpose behind the mystery.

> There was war in heaven. Michael fought against the *dragon*, not a beautiful archangel.

These verses describe a war in heaven in which Michael the archangel and his angels fight against the "dragon" and his angels. The dragon is clearly named as Satan in verse 9. Note that the war was with the dragon, not a beautiful archangel. Verse 9 also calls him that "ancient serpent." So at the time of his ejection, he already had experience as a serpent. It wasn't a new nature or identity that he acquired after losing his old job. Snakelike deception has always been his M.O., even when he spent time in heaven.

Also notice that the dragon did not fight against God but against Michael. And it appears that Satan did not initiate this battle as attempt to overthrow God. Rather, *Michael* started the war and the dragon and his angels "fought back" (verse 7).

He was hurled to earth, verse 9 says. Verse 8 says Satan and his demons "lost their place in heaven." Aha! They *did* have a place in heaven! But what was that place? As the worship leader? The answer comes up in a few verses, but let's first answer the question of when this happened.

In verse 10, a voice from heaven said, "Now have come the salvation and the power and the kingdom of our God, and the authority of his Christ" (NIV). When did salvation come, and when did the authority of Christ come? Salvation was secured in the death and resurrection of Jesus, of course. His death—the death of the sinless Son of God—was the last sacrifice needed to forgive sins. Jesus came, not to do away with Old Testament law, but to fulfill it (Matthew 5:17). One of the ways He fulfilled it was by being the last acceptable blood-shedding sacrifice, and the only life-giving sacrifice for sin. No more do we need to sacrifice bulls and goats. Jesus' sacrifice was once for all.

Furthermore, the resurrection of Jesus is crucial. Without it, the story ends nobly but in defeat. With the resurrection, Jesus defeated the power of death, having already defeated the power of sin during His life. Sin and death have gone together since the Garden of Eden, and Jesus defeated them both. His resurrection power is available for us to defeat the power of sin (Romans 8:11, 1 Corinthians 15:17). His *death* gives us forgiveness from sin. His *resurrection* provides power to refrain from continuing a life of sin. Revelation 12:10 is a reference to the cross.

And when was authority given to Jesus? It's clear from the Gospels that He had authority during His ministry on earth and he shared this authority with His disciples to some extent. In Matthew 10:1, Jesus gave them authority specifically to cast out demons and to heal disease and sickness. John 17:2 says the Father gave Jesus authority over all *flesh*. The NIV says "authority over all people." No wonder He could heal at will. He was *authorized* to do so. He had authority over sickness and demonic influences in people's lives (their flesh) and He even had authority to judge and forgive sins while on earth (Matthew 9:6). But when did He receive this authority? The Bible doesn't tell us, but there are implications that something happened either during His baptism or after passing the test in the wilderness.

However, at the same time, Satan also had some authority.

In Luke's description of the temptation of Jesus he writes:

> [5] And the devil took him up and showed him all the kingdoms of the world in a moment of time, [6] and said to him, "To you I will give all this authority and their glory, for it has been delivered to me, and I give it to whom I will. [7] If you, then, will worship me, it will all be yours."
>
> [8] And Jesus answered him, "It is written, 'You shall worship the Lord your God, and him only shall you serve.'"
>
> Luke 4:5-8, ESV

Jesus did not deny Satan's claim to such authority. Instead, He rejected Satan's offer and disagreed with Satan's means to obtain that authority. Now why would Satan have any authority and how did he get it? To answer this, we need to go back to the Beginning. When God created the earth, he gave Adam authority over the planet. The word in Genesis 1:28-30 is "dominion." In other words, Adam was given authority to run the planet and to rule over all the beasts. But when he followed the instruction of one of the beasts (the serpent), he gave away his authority to the beast. Satan, using tricky logic in the mouth of a serpent, deceived Eve and she influenced her husband and he rebelled against God's direction. Since Adam followed Satan's suggestion instead of obeying God's command, he forfeited the authority God had given him and gave it to Satan.

In the Bible, authority is always *given*. Jesus was given authority to do His ministry while on earth as seen in these verses:

Matthew 9:8...........Jesus was given authority to heal.

John 5:27 ...............The Father gave Jesus authority to judge.

John 17:2 ...............The Father gave Jesus authority over all people so He could give eternal life.

Matthew 28:18.......All authority was given to Jesus.

Jesus then gave this authority to His disciples to do ministry:

Matthew 10:1.........Jesus gave the Twelve authority to drive out evil spirits and heal diseases (repeated in Mark 6:7 and Luke 9:1).

Matthew 28:19.......Jesus transferred authority to His disciples when He commanded them to go and disciple the nations (this is discussed in more detail in chapter eight).

Luke 10:19.............Jesus gave seventy-two disciples authority over all the power of the enemy.

After the death and resurrection of Jesus, authority was and still is given to believers:

John 1:12 ...............Jesus gives authority to become God's children (most English Bibles say "right" or "power," though the literal Greek says "authority").

2 Corinthians 10:8.The Lord gave Paul authority to build up the church (repeated in 2 Corinthians 13:10).

Rev 2:26.................Jesus gives authority over the nations.

Authority is not given just for "spiritual" work or for "positive" purposes. Consider these other examples:

Rev 6:8 ................... Death, riding a pale horse, was given authority (most English Bibles say "power") over one-fourth of the earth to kill by a variety of means.

Rev 9:3 ................... "Locusts" were given authority to torture unbelievers.

John 19:11 .............. The civil authority which Pilate had as governor was given to him by God.

Luke 4:6 ................. Satan had been given authority over the kingdoms of the world. This authority (or "dominion") was given to him, by mistake, from Adam. Even Satan admitted that it was given to him. He didn't take it, steal it, or earn it. Adam witlessly handed it over.

Authority is always given. It's never taken or stolen. Adam was deceived into giving his dominion to Satan. From that point on, Satan had some control of the planet. In a sense, Satan won this authority fair and square. He didn't steal it. Sure, he lied about the whole thing, but Adam and Eve openly chose to believe that lie and follow Satan's bidding, ignoring the command of the Lord. They weren't forced or coerced into it. They were deceived, but they made the choice to do what they did. And when they made that choice, they traded the authority God gave them for a fruit snack. When they ate it, Satan obtained some authority, particularly in the area of death, which was a new concept.

> Authority is always *given*. It's never taken or stolen.

Since man gave away his authority, only a man could regain it. God was not about to *take* authority away from Satan and give it back to man, because authority is never *taken*, only *given*. So how could Jesus regain this authority? Satan would have known that the mission of Jesus would have included winning back the authority Adam had foolishly given away.

So Satan *tempted* Him with it: "I have some authority that I can give to whomever I choose. Would *you* like it?" This offer was not a benevolent act on his part. Like everything Satan says it was based on a lie and deception. If Jesus *had* worshiped him, he wouldn't have given Jesus any authority. Instead, Jesus would have become his slave like the rest of humanity. Jesus didn't fall for it like Adam did. He didn't take the bait. He would have to wait for the Father's timing to gain *all* authority.

That opportunity came after the Resurrection, when things changed significantly. In Matthew 28:18, Jesus informed the disciples of a new development in the authority business: "All authority in heaven and on earth has been given to me." The implication is that prior to this time He didn't have all authority, but now He did. Why was the cross such a defeat for Satan? It has to do with what Satan was "authorized" to do with the weapon of death; that is, whom he had the right to kill. From the time of Adam, Satan has had the right to kill those who follow him (i.e., "sinners"). Those who sin (that's everybody) follow Satan willingly and become his property—his slaves. As his property he has the *right* (authority) to kill them. And so he has done. It usually takes years to take effect, but Satan has dealt a deathblow to everyone who ever lived. That was the rule: People sin, Satan kills them. Sin brings death. God told Adam that the day he ate of the tree would be the day he died. Adam did die spiritually that day, but another death also began its process that day—physical death. When Adam sinned, his body became susceptible to disease and deterioration that led to death many years later. Sin and death have always gone hand in hand. *Death* in Scripture simply means "separation." Physical death is the *separation* of the spirit from the body. Spiritual death is *separation* from God. Eternal death is hell—forever separated from God's presence.

But when Satan killed Jesus, he violated the rules. He killed someone who wasn't his property. Jesus never sinned. Satan violated the order of things when he killed someone who was not his property. In that act, he forfeited his rights (authority) to wield death. In Revelation 1:18, Jesus said *He* now holds the keys to death and Hades. Satan forfeited the authority he had gained from the first Adam and gave it to the "last Adam" (1 Corinthians 15:45). Jesus won it back. All authority was given back to Him.

OK, all that to point out that all authority was given to Jesus at His death and resurrection. Whatever authority Satan had prior to that was forfeited. The phrase in Revelation 12:10, "Now have come…the authority of his Christ," is talking about all authority being given to Jesus (Matthew 28:18). Again, this verse is speaking of the death and resurrection of Jesus. It's in this context that Satan was cast down; that is, the casting down was in relation to the earthly life and ministry of Jesus.

Some have suggested that this could not be the case because verse 12 says Satan has gone down to the earth and knows that "his time [on earth] is short." The argument is that Satan must still have some place somewhere in the heavenlies and hasn't been hurled out yet, but when he does he won't be on the earth for long. This interpretation is dependent on the understanding of the word *short*. The Greek word translated "short" (*oligos*) is used to describe a small number of something—"a few." It is used forty-three times in the New Testament and most of the time it numbers or quantifies people, things, distances or concepts (e.g., he who forgives *little* loves *little*). About 20% of the time, it was used for describing a short period of time.[24] When used with time references, it means "a little while."

A literal understanding of the Greek word would support a view that Satan hasn't been hurled down yet, because "short" could hardly be considered 2,000 years—the time elapsed since the cross. However, we must be aware that expressions about lengths of time are relative, unless specifically quantified in hours, days or years. To a child, "short" means fifteen minutes. To the elderly, fifteen *years* is short. For a child, *a long time ago*, is probably a few months, since that represents a major portion of his life. To an older person, *a long time ago* is several years (depending on one's definition of "several"). To an historian, *a long time ago* is probably hundreds or thousands of years hence. One's age and perspective has a lot to do with quantifying time.

Consider God's perspective. He's been around an awfully long time. He's not even subject to time. He dwells in eternity, where there are no clocks. How He views time is not at all how we view time. I think this is what Peter was getting at in 1 Peter 3:8-9 where he says that God is not slow in keeping His promises. In other words, God is not delayed or negligent about them. He then goes on to say that for God, one day is like a thousand years. In other words, He is not affected by the passage of time like we are. This is also seen in Revelation 22:7, 12 where Jesus told John He is coming back *quickly*. This particular Greek word (*tachu*) occurs twelve times in the New Testament and was almost always used to describe timing that would be considered immediate.

So, if we conclude from Revelation 12 that Satan's "short" time cannot be the 2,000 years (or two "days") since Jesus' earthly ministry, then we are forced to admit that Jesus already came back and we missed it, since He told John He's coming quickly (or "immediately"). On the contrary, Jesus hasn't come back yet, though He is coming "quickly." While we wait for His return, we are forced to deal with Satan during this "short" time.

Let's turn now to discuss what Satan's place in heaven was. The second half of verse 10 describes him as the Accuser: "The accuser of our brothers, who accuses them before our God day and night, has been hurled down." I don't see worship leading there. I see an accuser. If we take these verses at face value, then Satan's role in heaven, before the cross, was the Accuser. In other words, he was still hanging around, accusing people before the Father, until the cross of Christ eliminated his position. Is there any other Scriptural evidence of this? Consider the story of Job. In Job 1 and 2, we read a curious story in which the "sons of God" (NIV says "angels" but the literal Hebrew is "sons of God") presented themselves before God, and Satan was with them (Job 1:6). The English name "Satan" comes directly from the Hebrew word *satan*. It means an adversary—one who withstands. A related noun, *sitna* means "enmity," or "accusation." In this story, we see Satan functioning as both an adversary and an accuser.

God asks Satan what he thinks of Job, and thus begins a chess match in heaven. God gives Satan permission to test Job multiple times and in multiple ways, before Satan is defeated and Job vindicated at the end of the book. In the first two chapters of Job, Satan accuses (or slanders) Job before God as being faithful only because God handed him life on a silver platter. "Take the silver platter away," Satan says, "and see if he still serves you." So Satan took the silver platter away but Job still remained faithful to God. (I hope you realize there was some major paraphrasing going on there!)

We see another example of Satan's accusation of people before God in Zechariah 3:1. Joshua the high priest stood before God, and Satan stood at the side accusing him. But the Lord rebuked Satan and had Joshua clothed in clean garments to illustrate his removal of sin and guilt, signified by the filthy garments he had been wearing.

Satan, it would seem, still had access to heaven, and had audiences with God *after* the alleged ejection from heaven and casting to the earth prior to the Garden of Eden. That place Satan had in heaven was to accuse people before God. And in a sense, he had reason to. They were all guilty of sin with no permanent atonement available. But that all changed at the cross, where Jesus' one-time-fits-all sacrifice provided the means for forgiveness.

The word "accuser" in Revelation 12:10 occurs seven times in the New Testament. In all the other occurrences, it's used in a legal sense. For example, in John 8 a woman was accused of adultery and was about to receive the penalty prescribed in the Law of Moses. And when Paul found himself in a legal battle in the Roman court system, his opponents were referred to as "accusers" five times in Acts 23 to 25. For example, Festus said in Acts 25:16, "It is not the Roman custom to hand over any man before he has faced his accusers and has had an opportunity to defend himself against their charges." This is the word John used to describe Satan in Revelation 12:10—a word usually used in a courtroom setting. We might describe that role as a *prosecuting attorney*. Remember that. It's important.

On the other hand, 1 John 2:1 describes Jesus as an "advocate" who speaks to the Father in our defense. The word "advocate" is the Greek word *parakletos*, where we get the English word "Paraclete," usually used in reference to the Holy Spirit. In secular settings, *parakletos* was used to describe someone who testified in court in behalf of someone.[25] We would call that person a "witness." There was also a technical meaning, used rarely, where *parakletos* meant an attorney. We might describe that role as a *defense attorney*. Remember that, too. It's even more important

So here's the great news: Because of the cross, Satan no longer has any evidence to bring before God with which to accuse us. Instead of an *accuser* standing before the Father, we have

| Satan's role in heaven as prosecuting attorney has been replaced by Jesus as defense attorney. |

an *Advocate*: Jesus Christ. *Satan's role in heaven as prosecuting attorney has been replaced by Jesus as defense attorney!* Jesus is now there to intercede for us (Hebrews 7:25). That's exactly what Job was wishing for in Job 9:33 when he said, "If only there were someone to arbitrate between us" (him and God). This wish was, of course, fulfilled in Jesus and described in 1 Timothy 2:5, "There is one God and one mediator between God and men, the man Christ Jesus."

That's great news, but there's a catch. Satan was cast down in Revelation 12:10, but he landed where we live. So we have to put up with him being here full time. He still remains the Accuser, but God will no longer listen to the garbage he has to say. So instead, Satan accuses us to our faces. Haven't we all experienced that! "You did that, and you call yourself a Christian! You'll never amount to anything! You should be ashamed. You've really done it this time. You've gone too far—you can never go back. Loser! Failure! etc, etc." The list of lies goes on and on, but the point is that he is now forced to accuse us directly, because he lost his place in heaven and God won't listen to it anymore.

### Jude 6. "Angels that abandoned their positions."

The book of Jude is such an interesting little book. Or can I say unusual? It contains some things that aren't found anywhere else in Scripture. Jude says he wanted to write an encouraging letter about God's salvation, but because of all the frauds and false teaching in the church, he had to speak out on the problem of rebellion, especially when it occurs in the church. Jude begins in verse 4 by pointing out that there are imposters who have sneaked into the church and are spreading false doctrines and ungodly attitudes.

To illustrate this, Jude provides three examples of something good gone bad. The first example is the Israelites. Even though they were delivered from Egypt, some were later destroyed because they didn't believe (verse 5). Another example is Sodom and Gomorrah, who were destroyed because of their immorality (verse 7). But in verse 6, a bazaar example: "And the angels who did not keep their positions of authority but abandoned their own home—these he has kept in darkness, bound with everlasting chains for judgment on the great Day."

The first part of this verse certainly seems to suggest a Lucifer-type fall. They didn't keep their authority but abandoned their home. However, the last part raises a question. If this verse refers to Satan and his demons, how can Jude say they are already bound and kept in darkness until the "great Day"?

There are a few problems with interpreting this verse as the fall of Lucifer. First, there is no other clear Biblical reference of angels who didn't keep their authority but abandoned their home. Secondly, these angels don't appear to be *stripped* of authority and *evicted* from their home. Rather, they *didn't keep* their authority, and *they abandoned* their home. Thirdly, Satan and his demons are not bound in darkness; they are running around causing me trouble. Their day of punishment is yet to come, as described in Revelation 20:10 and Isaiah 24:21. And finally, this passage is hard to understand, because, well, it's Jude.

Jude is a tough nut to crack. For example, verse 9 describes the battle over the body of Moses between Michael and Satan. Weird, huh? Nowhere else in the Bible is this event described.[26] Deuteronomy 34:6 says Moses was not buried by a man and that no man knew where he was buried. The text simply says "he" buried Moses. Most of us have assumed that "he" is God, but no mention is made in Deuteronomy of an angelic fight over Moses' body. The point is, Jude brings up some unusual things and figuring them out isn't necessary to understand the main point of Jude, which is, "Watch out for rebellious imposters in the church!" If it isn't necessary to understand the details of Jude's unusual examples in order to understand Jude's thesis, I suggest not being too dogmatic about deciphering the details.

However, if you backed me into a corner and forced me to confess an opinion on what Jude is talking about, this is what I would say: I think the angels in Jude 6 are the "sons of God" who became sexually active with human women as recorded in Genesis 6:4. (That text is discussed below.) The reason I think this is because Jude appears to be referring to the book of 1 Enoch, which goes into detail about this weird crossbreeding.

The book of 1 Enoch, like 2 Enoch (see previous chapter), is part of the pseudepigrapha. Enoch was the great-grandfather of Noah and was the man who "was not for God took him" (Genesis 5:24). Enoch certainly did not write the books which bear his name, but the scribe(s) who wrote them down were probably working off an oral tradition about Enoch's life. It's interesting stuff, but most of us would not view it as inspired or even historically accurate. However, the Ethiopian Orthodox Church trusts 1 Enoch enough to include it in the canon of their Bible. Apparently, Jude valued the book as well and was not afraid to quote from it, which he does explicitly eight verses later:

> It was also about these that Enoch, the seventh from Adam, prophesied, saying, "Behold, the Lord comes with ten thousands of his holy ones, to execute judgment on all and to convict all the ungodly of all their deeds of ungodliness that they have committed in such an ungodly way, and of all the harsh things that ungodly sinners have spoken against him."
> —Jude 14, 15, ESV

This is a direct quote of 1 Enoch 1:9. If Jude quotes it here, I'm assuming he would have no problem referring to it in verse

6, where 1 Enoch provides more commentary on the sin of the angels in Genesis 6:4. If this is the case, Jude is definitely not talking about the fall of Lucifer.

## 2 Peter 2:4. "Angels sent to hell."

A similar passage to Jude 6 is the one found in 2 Peter 2:4. Like Jude, Peter is addressing the problem of false prophets. And like Jude, Peter lists several examples in verses 4 through 8 of how God rescues the godly and punishes the wicked. One of the examples he cites is that God didn't spare angels when they sinned. Instead, He sent them to hell, putting them in "gloomy dungeons" (NIV) to be held until they are judged. Like the Jude passage, we can't know for certain who these angels are or what they did. Unless we believe that hell is on earth, then this could not be a reference to Lucifer's rebellion, because in that scenario Lucifer was sent to earth, not hell.

## The "Sons of God" of Genesis 6:1-4

This, then, is the text that 1 Enoch refers to, and which I'm suggesting is what the Jude and 2 Peter texts are referring to:

> [1] When man began to multiply on the face of the land and daughters were born to them, [2] the sons of God saw that the daughters of man were attractive. And they took as their wives any they chose. [3] Then the LORD said, "My Spirit shall not abide in man forever, for he is flesh: his days shall be 120 years." [4] The Nephilim were on the earth in those days, and also afterward, when the sons of God came in to the daughters of man and they bore children to them. These were the mighty men who were

of old, the men of renown.
—ESV

There are scads of theories about this one, and I'll add mine
to them. Please understand that this is a *theory*. If you meet
someone who thinks he has a complete handle on this one,
don't let him date your daughter. I don't believe anyone can
fully explain this unusual text. But that shouldn't stop us from
having an interesting discussion and sharing theories.

These verses tell the story of how the "sons of God" noticed
how attractive human women were and decided to marry them.
They produced amazing offspring. Who were these "sons of
God"? Were these demons or angels or great men? The text
seems to point to them being some sort of non-human, spiritual
beings, and not very nice ones at that. They are called "sons
of God," in a similar vein as Job 1:6 when the "sons of God"
(among them, Satan) appeared before God. Some Bible
translations say "angels" instead of "sons of God," which may
or may not make it clearer to the reader. Both the angels and the
demons are referred to as sons of God because they are members
of God's creation. God is their "Father" through creation, but
not through redemption or by their character. For that matter,
every human being is a child of God in the creation sense (see
Acts 17:28), but only those who have repented and are obedient
to the Gospel of Jesus through faith are children of God in a
spiritual sense and relate to God as Father through adoption.
As it turns out, God didn't appreciate his "spirit-children"
marrying up with humans, so He said that His Spirit would not
contend with man forever. In other words, it's not appropriate
to mix spirit and flesh in that way. Perhaps this was the angelic
sin that Jude and Peter were referring to. It doesn't answer all
the questions we might have, but the Bible just doesn't provide
a lot of information on this.

Job 4:18 has a similar thought. Eliphaz the Temanite says that God "charges His angels with error." Eliphaz also argues that the "holy ones" cannot be trusted and the heavens are not pure in His eyes (Job 15:15). These references could certainly support a Lucifer rebellion (if that were clearly described in Scripture), but they could also point to the failure of the "sons of God" in Genesis 6. But before we begin to build too much doctrine on these references from Job, let's consider who is talking and why he said it. Job's friend Eliphaz is the speaker, and he is trying to convince Job that Job's predicament was caused by his sin against God. Job insists on maintaining his innocence, but Eliphaz says, "Hey, if even the angels mess up, who do you think you are, claiming to be innocent?" Keep in mind that the book of Job does not quote Eliphaz because he has everything figured out. In fact, he was dead wrong on his judgment of Job! And what does he mean by the heavens not being pure? If he means the dwelling place of God, he's wrong again.

I think we have to conclude that Eliphaz's opinions can't be trusted. At the end of the book, God tells Eliphaz, "I am angry with you and your two friends, because you have not spoken of me what is right, as my servant Job has" (Job 42:7). Perhaps it was Eliphaz's flippant comment about heaven's purity that angered God. I don't know if anyone tries to use Eliphaz's argument as evidence of fallen angels, but who could seriously recommend using Eliphaz the Temanite as a source of sound doctrine? Especially such a short, fleeting comment buried in a sea of other comments that God later rebuffs?

We may not be able to precisely identify the mischievous "sons of God" of Genesis 6, but the timing of their error cannot be linked to the traditional Lucifer-rebellion story. Lucifer's alleged rebellion occurred prior to any population of the earth, since Satan was already present in the Garden of Eden tempting Eve. But the error of these spirits was committed *on earth* (not heaven) long after the supposed fall of Lucifer.

## 1 Peter 3:19-20. Jesus Preached to Spirits in Prison

Once again, Peter drops a short bit of confusing information in 1 Peter 3:19-20. Some have connected this passage to others we have looked at in Jude and 2 Peter. The idea is that Jesus, after His death, descended into Hades and preached to the demons that were sent there. Once again, this could hardly be a reference to fallen angels, because the Lucifer theory says fallen angels fell to the Earth, not Hades.

It's difficult to support a view that some fallen angels were assigned to earth and others were sent to "prison" (hell). Peter doesn't completely explain these events, but it's more likely that the "spirits" that Jesus preached to are the spirits of the not-so-dearly-departed folks that lived during the time of Noah. Certainly they were disobedient, and their disobedience determined their destination after death. Apparently, Jesus spent some time with them explaining their error before the final judgment. A bazaar story, to be sure, but not useful to support the traditional view of a Lucifer rebellion.

## Isaiah 24:21. Punishment of the Exalted Ones

This is not a verse that is typically used to discuss Lucifer's fall from heaven, but I mention it to illustrate how prevalent assumptions about Lucifer are and how those assumptions— presumptions, actually—interfere with reasonable Bible interpretation. The NIV renders this verse like this:

> In that day the LORD will punish the powers in
> the heavens above and the kings on the earth
> below.

The NKJV translates "powers" as "exalted ones." But here's the kicker, and this is why I included this verse in this chapter: I was minding my own business, doing my devotions one day and reading from the New Living Translation, when I stumbled across this verse. The NLT renders "powers" as "fallen angels." Whoa! Let's talk about that for a minute. The word "fallen" does *not* appear in the text. The Hebrew word (*marom*) means *height, elevated place*, or *on high*. It usually refers to God's rank and position, but could be used of others in a negative sense, as in "haughty." In this verse, the word appears twice, back to back: *ha-marom ba-marom*. A literal translation could say, "the elevated ones on high."

I like to read the NLT, because it's easy and fun to read and I don't trip on phrases that are clumsy or have to pause for words not used in every day speech. But here is an example of how Bible translators' bias or presuppositions can affect how they do the interpretive part of their translation work. (And don't let anyone kid you; *every* translation has some interpretation and paraphrasing in order to make the English readable, even the most literal translations.) *If* there were "fallen angels," then this *might* be an appropriate interpretation of the verse. But I'm arguing that there are no fallen angels that reside in either heaven or earth. There are the mystery spirits that Jude and Peter describe that are being held in prison for judgment later on. And there are evil spirits that do Satan's bidding here on earth. But I don't believe they fell from heaven as a result of a muffed coup incited by Lucifer's rebellion.

I bring up this verse because it's a great example of how prevalent the thinking about Lucifer and fallen angels is. Here are learned Bible scholars who have ventured off the road of literal translation and have imposed an interpretation based on something "everybody knows"—everyone except the early church fathers! It is a doctrine that cannot be satisfactorily supported by Scripture. It's a doctrine that raises more questions than it answers.

## There's *Still* Some Explaining to do!

Up to this point, I have challenged the doctrine of Lucifer and offered some alternative interpretations to the commonly used proof-texts. However, I have also raised some questions that I haven't answered. I will try to begin answering some of those questions in the next chapter. For example, *If Satan has always been evil, what was God thinking when He created him?* And, *If God created Satan evil, did God create evil?* Great questions! Read on, my friend, and let's see how we do.

## CHAPTER SIX
## SO WHERE DID EVIL COME FROM?

*I* have been challenging the idea that Satan existed first as Lucifer, a beautiful angel with significant responsibility in heaven who made a celestial power play and got the axe. I'm challenging this idea because the Scriptures we have used to support this notion do not clearly say what we have been so clearly taught. There are some verses, however, that do very clearly describe Satan's background.

1 John 3:8 says, "The devil has been sinning from the beginning." John 8:44 says the devil "was a murderer from the beginning, and does not stand in the truth, because there is no truth in him. When he speaks a lie, he speaks from his own resources, for he is a liar and the father of it" (NKJV). If the devil has been sinning and murdering since "the beginning," doesn't it sound like he has *always* been evil—that there was never a time he wasn't evil? I guess that depends on what "since the beginning" means. Does it mean *Satan's* beginning or the beginning of the *world*? Was he good at one time but started lying and murdering before the world began, or has he always been evil since his own beginning?

The phrase "in the beginning" is used over twenty times in the New Testament. With each one of these occurrences, the context usually makes it obvious which beginning is being discussed. The best interpretation of the phrase in 1 John 3:8 and John 8:44, when compared with other uses of "in the beginning" in the New Testament, would seem to refer to *Satan's* beginning. In other words, since *his* beginning he has been a murderer and a liar. He has *always* been so. He did not begin as a good angel and let his success go to his head. He was created void of God's presence and goodness, and having only the attribute of Self, he turned inward (opposite of love) and began to plan deeds based on hate.

John 8:44 says when Satan lies, he speaks from "his own resources" (NKJV). Literally, the Greek reads, "When he (Satan) speaks a lie, he speaks from his own."[27] In other words, when Satan speaks a lie he is speaking out of who he is—a liar. That's his nature and character—the *true* representation of his *false* personality. The phrase suggests a way of existing that has always been. It's who he is. There's no indication that he was ever something else.

These verses state pretty clearly that the character of Satan has always been evil. He was not created good and then went bad. If he was created good then rebelled, as the popular doctrine claims, then there are some serious questions to answer:

1. When we go to heaven, can we rebel and go bad, too? Are we safe in heaven? If Satan could go bad, without a tempter to tempt him (he became the tempter), then can that happen to us, too?

2. How is it possible to rebel, to become filled with self (the essence of pride) while in the very presence of the Holy God?

3. Why didn't God destroy the devil when he rebelled? Why did he send him to the Earth to mess up Adam's paradise?

These questions are a bit of a frustration for most Christians who believe the theory of Lucifer's rebellion. But if we reject the Lucifer story and believe that Satan has always been evil, we still have a serious question to answer: Did God create evil? I'm going to give a crack at answering this question in this chapter.

One theory is that evil does not exist as a character trait, like goodness does. Rather, evil is merely the *absence* of a character trait: God's goodness. In Exodus 33:18-19 Moses wanted to see God's glory. Instead, God said He would let His *goodness* pass before Moses. God's goodness is and has substance. But evil is not a something. It's an adjective describing the absence of God's goodness. A creature, completely void of God's goodness, turns in on itself and becomes evil. I'm suggesting that Satan was created completely void of God's presence, goodness and character (holiness). Not even man, as depraved as we are, was created evil. Romans 3:23, Jeremiah 17:9, Psalms 14:2-3 and others say that everyone has sinned and that we are all evil, but this is not how it was at the creation. God said of the creation of the world, "It is good." Adam was part of that creation and therefore was created good. However, we have all gone our own way (Isaiah 53:6) and become corrupted. It would appear from the 1 John 3 and John 8 texts that Satan never became corrupted, because he always existed in a state void of goodness.

Consider an illustration from nature. Think of the difference between light and dark. Technically, there is no darkness. There is only the absence of light. Light, by scientific definition, is electromagnetic radiation with wavelengths that are visible to the eye (*visible* light). When all visible light is absent, we experience darkness. Darkness isn't a something, like light is. *Dark* is just a description for the condition in which no light is present.

In the same way, cold is not a something that exists. It's just the absence of heat. When we describe something as being cold, we are simply stating that its temperature is less than something else is. Heat is relative and we use temperatures for comparison. In Minnesota, where I live, we have a different definition for cold than someone who lives in Florida. Similarly, Minnesotans' definitions of hot and cold change with the seasons. We would say 40° is "cold" in August, but that same temperature would be "warm" in January. "Cold" is a description of the relative absence of heat. Heat, on the other hand, is a something. It can be measured (in degrees) and there is no limit to the amount of heat that can be generated; you can always strike another match. But there *is* a limit to cold. Remove all heat, and you have absolute zero (about –460° F), the temperature in outer space, where there is absolutely no heat source.

Are these illustrations from nature fair comparisons to the relationship between good and evil? Maybe they are, considering some of the metaphors the Bible uses to describe the nature of God. The Bible says God is light, and there is no darkness in Him whatsoever (1 John 1:5). The Scripture frequently compares the relationship between good and evil with light and darkness (e.g., Isaiah 9:2, John 1:5, 3:19, 8:12, and many others). Coincidence? Or is the Bible giving us some hints about the nature of evil compared to goodness, a quality that belongs to God alone but He shares with those who believe in Him?

Consider also that Deuteronomy 4:24 and Hebrews 12:29 refer to God as being a "consuming *fire*." Fire is a heat *and* light source. Another coincidental comparison? Or is it another clue?

If this theory is correct and these analogies are appropriate, then an important distinction can be drawn between good and evil and between God and Satan. If evil is a description of the lack of goodness and doesn't really exist as a something, then Satan cannot invent new forms of evil. We talk about how bad things are getting, as if Satan's endless creativity is devising new ways to sin. But Satan isn't a creator. God is the Creator, and He created *man* in His image.

Satan was not created in God's image. In the *Creator's* image, *man* has creative ability, though limited. We cannot create matter out of nothing, as God can, but we can take God's building blocks, and with creative ability we can invent new things. Satan cannot create anything, not even evil. He can only pervert what God has created. God does something new. Satan perverts it. It appears to be a new form of evil, but it's simply a distortion of something new that God has done.

So did God create evil when He created Satan? I would say "no," simply because evil cannot be created. It is a distortion or absence of goodness. Satan is sort of a "vacuum spirit," sucking up and spitting out whatever is in his path and not tied down. John 10:10 says the devil is a *thief* (taker, not giver), *killer* (taker of life, not giver of life), and *destroyer* (exterminator, not creator). He is a vacuum spirit—empty, frustrated, and devoid of God's holiness. His evil schemes are attempts to undo the good that God has created. Evil is not a thing to be feared. It is a nothing, imposed on the world by an uncreative illusionist. Only God is to be feared, and His goodness is to be enjoyed as something real and tangible.

Jack Hayford makes an excellent point that serves as a good example of Satan's perversions of God's creations. Consider why the devil has perverted sexuality so much. In one sense, he has targeted sex because it is the most intimate expression of love between a man and a woman. If he can cause dysfunction in that relationship, it will wreck lives and families, erode society and introduce death (separation) through abortion, adultery, divorce, depression, suicide, etc.

Another reason Satan targets sexuality is to disrupt husband-wife relationships, because marriage is a picture of Christ and the church (Ephesians 5:23-25, 32) and he hates anything that reminds him of the relationship we can have with Jesus. Yet another reason he aims to pervert human sexuality is because it is through sexual relations that life is begotten. Satan cannot create or beget human life. He hates that he can't. It's an ability that only God possesses, and to a degree He shares that ability with us. Satan hates life and life-producing activity. So he attempts to distort and pervert sexual intimacy.[28]

In the same way, Satan is the corrupter of everything the Creator has invented. When a new expression of godliness is expressed through God's people, Satan will immediately get to work to counterfeit, pervert, or destroy it. The results of his labor is not a new evil, it's a perversion of a new expression of godliness (goodness).

## Does Satan have a choice in the matter?

In Genesis, we are told that God created man (i.e., human beings) in His image. It does not say in what image the spirit beings were created. Among some of the obvious differences between humans and spirits (both angelic and demonic spirits), I want to point out a difference that has significance for this discussion.

Humans, like God, have the ability to make choices. With some restrictions, we can generally say that we are able to decide what to eat for breakfast. We can decide if and whom we'll marry. We can decide what career we'll pursue. We can also decide whether we will choose to follow Christ or reject the calling of the Holy Spirit. If we choose to follow Christ, we can then choose what church to go to and whether we'll sin today or not. Of course, these are simplifications of complicated matters, but ultimately it boils down to choices we make.[29]

The Scriptures do not give any evidence that spirit-beings have that same ability to make choices. Human beings have fallen but are redeemable. Demonic beings are not redeemable.

Their fate has been sealed. It's just a matter of time before judgment comes and they are sent to hell. (Incidentally, hell—that is, "everlasting fire," Matthew 25:41—was created for Satan and his demons, not for sinners.) I suggest to you that not only are spirit-beings not capable of receiving redemption from the shed blood of Christ, they are neither capable of repentance *nor* disobedience. In the following chapters, I'll discuss the purpose that Satan and his demons serve in God's design, but for now let me illustrate what I'm talking about with a Scriptural example.

In Mark 1:27, Jesus gave a command to a demon that was tormenting an individual, and the demon obeyed Him. This completely amazed the crowd. Here was a guy that taught with authority, not the dry, wimpy teaching they were used to. And Jesus packed a punch. When He gave the word, the demons obeyed. OK, let's pause right there. Think about it. The demons *obeyed* Him. Do you find that a bit interesting? Not even Christians always do that! Demons obeying Jesus should seem really weird to us, because the Great Commission teaches that the essence of being a Christian is to obey Christ (Matthew 28:20). The disciples were taught to make disciples of others by teaching them to obey everything He taught them. So if the demons obeyed Him, why didn't that make them Christians? Especially when not even Christians are always obedient?

The answer to this question (and then I'll make my point) is that in the Great Commission, the Greek word translated "obey" (or "observe") means *to keep, pay attention to, keep under guard, maintain,* or *keep firm.*[30] In Mark 1, the word the demons obeyed with is a different word[31] that meant *be subject to.* This isn't an obedience that stems from love and the desire to serve. This is a forced obedience that comes from fear. They clearly could not disobey. They had no choice in the matter. Though demons are allowed to run amuck in this world, when

God gives the word, they must obey! It would seem from this and other examples of Jesus and His disciples interacting with demons, that angelic spirits—whether heavenly or hellish—do not have the freedom to choose or reject obedience, as people do. God gives commands to people and we have the choice to obey and reap the benefits, or disobey and suffer the consequences.

The spirit world does not have that option. Satan may rebel against God's principles, but he cannot rebel against God's command.

> Satan may rebel against God's *principles*, but he cannot rebel against God's *command*.

This is particularly encouraging to us because *when we speak God's word in the authority, power and leading of the Holy Spirit, demons must obey*. The disciples experienced this, and were amazed by it (Luke 10:17).

In the next chapter, we'll explore the reasons why Satan exists and the purpose he serves in God's design. Psalm 119:91 says "all things serve you (God)," or, "all are Your servants." The Hebrew word "all" in this verse refers to "everything," and when it appears by itself, as in this verse, it usually means "all of creation,"[32] as in, "His kingdom rules over all" (Psalm 103:19). Since Satan is part of all created things, we know that he serves a function in God's plan. Satan's evil intent actually contributes to God's good plan. Satan's evil intent wasn't even his choice. He was created the way he is and he had no choice in the matter. Unfair for him, you say? Look, let's not waste any pity on Satan and his demons. Though he has a purpose in God's design, it would appear that he has abused his role, having taken it much too far, and therefore deserves no pity. He was created as a "vessel of destruction" as described in Romans 9.

God, in His wisdom and sovereignty, has created certain beings to be objects of His mercy and others to be objects of His wrath. But that doesn't excuse the objects of wrath from their personal responsibility and evil. Remember, *God* hardened Pharaoh's heart for His purpose, but when you read the story it certainly appears that Pharaoh was just being stubborn without any help from God.

There are different ways of trying to explain this. If you believe in the free will of man separate from God's control (Arminian theology), you might say that Pharaoh was being stubborn, so God hardened his heart because of his rebellion. If you reject man's free will and believe that God controls our choices (Calvinism), you would probably say that Pharaoh was predestined for that purpose. So to achieve that purpose, God hardened his heart. I'm not going to pick sides in that issue because that's not my purpose. Let me simply point out what the two sides have in common:

- Both agree that God hardened Pharaoh's heart. They may not agree about "who started it," but it's clear that God made it harder for Pharaoh.
- Both would agree that Pharaoh was responsible for his actions. Pharaoh sinned against God and was deserving of God's wrath, even though (or if) he was predestined for that sin.

In Romans 9, Paul says that God has mercy on whom he wants to have mercy, and He hardens those He wants to harden. Paul answers the obvious question, "Then how can God blame us?" by flatly saying, "Who are you...to talk back to God?" (verses 18-20). If Paul is speaking about God's mercy and hardening of mankind, who has been given choices regarding sin and righteousness, it shouldn't be difficult to believe that God also created spirit-beings for a purpose—some for noble, some not so noble. Some were created for His wrath, just like Pharaoh.

Another example of demons strict obedience to the command of Christ is found in Mark 5:13. In that story, the demons had to ask Jesus for permission to enter the pigs. They didn't appear to have clearance to do whatever they wanted. They had to ask first. Demons do not have free rein to do whatever they want whenever they want. God is ultimately in control of everything.

### So if God didn't create 'evil,' why did He create Satan?

This chapter has begun to explore the origin of evil. We have considered that Satan was created in the state that he currently is—devoid of any godliness—giving him an evil nature. We have looked at Scriptures that seem to teach that evil spirits do not have the freedom to choose their behavior, but that they must do evil. They cannot repent.

However, when God gives the word (or when a Christian delivers God's word), demons must obey since they do not have the freedom to choose disobedience. What we haven't explored yet is why God would create beings that are void of His presence and goodness. What possible purpose could a good God hope to accomplish in creating beings that are not good? That's what the next chapter finally tackles.

# CHAPTER SEVEN
# REASONS FOR SATAN'S EXISTENCE

*T*he Lucifer theory says that Satan was created good but went bad, losing the good name Lucifer and being renamed Satan. If this were the case, we would have some questions to answer: Why didn't God destroy him when he rebelled? Why did God send him to earth and make our lives miserable? Why doesn't He banish him from the earth and keep him away from us permanently when we pray for spiritual victories?

For some reason, God allows Satan to stick around. Even when Jesus had opportunity to banish demons, He gave them a break and let them remain in the area. In Luke 8 when He was casting the Legion of demons out of a demoniac, the demons begged Him, "Don't send us to the abyss." It appears from the story that Jesus could have done that. But instead, Jesus allowed them to remain on the planet. He even allowed them to stay in the vicinity, as they had begged of Him in Mark's version of the story (Mark 5). Not only did He not send them to hell, the pit, the abyss or even Antarctica, He allowed them to remain locally. Why would He have done that? It's because Satan and his demons serve a purpose in God's plan. They have a reason for being here. Here are six reasons I have found in Scripture:

## 1. To carry out God's wrath on sinners.

God is a good God of love and grace. He is patient and slow to anger, wanting everyone to come to repentance (2 Peter 3:9). However, there are times when sin has gone so far that it must simply be judged here on earth before the sinner stands before God in eternity. It is for those times of judgment that God turns sinners over to demonic forces to be punished. In that way, God does not need to do it Himself.

Psalm 119:91 says all things serve God. Since demonic spirits are part of "all things," we must accept that even they have their role in serving God. Proverbs 16:4 also says that God has made everything, even the wicked, for Himself. In other words, everything—even demons—were created for His purpose. There is nothing that exists that doesn't fit into His plan. He created everything "on purpose."

So when the time comes for God to execute His wrath on the wicked, does He send the host of heaven to do it? Not necessarily! Psalm 109:6 says, "Appoint the evil one to oppose the evil man" (NIV). NKJV says, "Set a wicked man over him, and let an accuser stand at his right hand." The word "accuser" or "evil one" is actually the Hebrew word *satan*. This verse points out that God can use an evil person, perhaps even Satan himself, to carry out judgment on another evil person.

In Isaiah 54:16, God says He created "the destroyer" to "work havoc" (NIV). To *work havoc* means to destroy, spoil, or corrupt. Who is this Destroyer that God made to make a mess of things? The text doesn't say, but perhaps it's the same "destroyer" mentioned in Exodus 12:23, when the so-called angel of death struck down the first-born of Egypt. The same Hebrew word for destroyer is used in both verses. Whoever he/it is, God was the one who created a being called the Destroyer for a specific purpose for which he is named: destruction. Why would God make a being like this? Primarily, to carry out His judgment. Note that Isaiah doesn't say, "God made a decent angelic being that went along with Lucifer's rebellion and so now he's into corruption." No, God created the Destroyer to do destruction. The works of sinners, and sometimes sinners themselves, are occasionally met with God's judgment of destruction. For those instances, the Destroyer is deployed.

In the same vein, Revelation 9:13-15 tells us of a coming day of judgment in which four angels, who are currently bound at the Euphrates River, will be released to kill one third of mankind. These angels are not the type you would see with the shepherds at your Christmas pageant. Apparently, these angels are so fiercely destructive they have to be kept tied up until their appointed day. Their assignment is directed by a voice from heaven, presumably God's voice, and their mission is clearly one of judgment, according to the context of the chapter.

In the Old Testament there are several references describing how God used pagan kings and nations to teach Israel and Judah a lesson, or to carry out His judgment against them. These are examples of Psalm 109:6 and illustrate the role that evil beings (like demons) have in "serving" God. Consider these:

- ✓ In Isaiah 10:6-12 the king of Assyria is basically described as a military club in God's hand, though the king had no idea that he was doing God's plan. But because of the king's arrogance, God later punished him, after he had served God's purpose.

- ✓ Habakkuk 1:5 is often used as a verse of encouragement anticipating a new thing God might like to do in our midst, but that's not an appropriate interpretation of the verse. There are other Bible verses that speak encouraging words of God doing something new, as in Isaiah 43:18-19, but this verse in Habakkuk was more of a warning than encouragement. This new thing that God said would "utterly amaze" His people is that He would raise up the Babylonians to take the Jews captive! The reasons why He would do that are the same as those described above in the Isaiah 10 passage.

✓ In Jeremiah 25:9-14 (and 27:6) the Lord says, "My servant Nebuchadnezzar will destroy this land because of its wickedness, but later I will punish Babylon for *its* guilt." Note that Nebuchadnezzar, a pagan king, was called God's servant because God would use him to discipline His people. However, the Babylonians took the discipline too far and later had to be punished because of how they treated the Jews, which is seen in the next example.

✓ Zechariah 1:15 describes the nations used to discipline God's people, but these nations "over-did it." As in the above passages, they took the punishment too far and brought God's wrath back on themselves. This verse says God was only a "little angry" with His people, so He called upon other nations to punish them. But those nations went beyond what God had intended. They did help, "but with evil intent" (NKJV). The NIV says those nations just "added to the calamity." The NLT does some interpretive work and makes it obvious: "I am very angry with the other nations that enjoy peace and security. I was only a little angry with my people, but the nations punished them far beyond my intentions." So while God was only a "little angry" with His people, now He is "exceedingly angry" with the other nations.

In a similar way, Satan and his demons have taken God's wrath too far, and they will suffer eternally for it.

## 2. To discipline rebellious saints.

This is similar to the first one, except in this case the introduction of demonic disturbance in the life of a believer is not so much to judge them, but to "encourage" them to repent and come back to healthy, holy living. Again, God is a loving Father who doesn't take pleasure in the suffering of His children. But for those Christians who are rebellious, there are consequences.

Many people don't like the idea of God standing by with a big stick and whacking them on the head when they mess up. I don't like the idea either, and it would be hard to build a convincing argument from Scripture about God behaving that way. However, we do know that bad choices yield uncomfortable results. The decision to jump off a building yields negative results when the jumper returns to earth. Is God punishing the jumper for a bad choice? The Bible teaches that there are consequences for sinning. Those consequences are one aspect of what the Scriptures call *discipline*, which is intended for those God loves and those He accepts as His children (see Hebrews 12:6).

There is a cause-and-effect nature of the choices we make. When we make bad choices (disobedience) we step out from underneath God's protective covering, making us vulnerable to demonic attack. So it's not so much that God is getting back at us, or that He's telling the devil, "Sic 'em!" It's not even that He stopped blessing us. What actually happened was that we rejected His love, refused His blessings, and stepped out from underneath His protection when we disobeyed. The natural result of going outside in the rain without an umbrella is that we get wet. When we step out from underneath God's protective umbrella, the natural result is that we get hit. This is what Moses explained to the Israelites in Deuteronomy chapters 28 and 30:

*If you obey God, you will be blessed. If you disobey, you will be cursed. If you turn to God, you will prosper. You have the choice of life and death, so choose life.*

Micah 7:8-10 shows the consequences of sin yet also includes the hope of restoration. When Israel sinned, they abandoned God's protection and were fair game for the Enemy's assault. But after humbling themselves and enduring the consequences, Micah is convinced that God will come to their aid and judge in their favor. He says,

> Rejoice not over me, O my enemy; when I fall, I shall rise; when I sit in darkness, the LORD will be a light to me. I will bear the indignation of the LORD because I have sinned against him, until he pleads my cause and executes judgment for me. He will bring me out to the light; I shall look upon his vindication.
>
> Micah 7:8-9, ESV

There was complete awareness that their sin had caused them to fall and to be in darkness. Yet Micah expresses faith in God, so they could boldly tell the enemy they will rise from their fallen state and the Lord would bring them out to the light. Micah understands that they must endure God's "indignation" because of the sin, but that once the judgment is over, God will execute judgment and vindication in their favor. The lesson to these verses is that the one who sins steps away from God's protection. The Lord's indignation allows the Enemy to have some fun ("rejoicing"), but following humility and repentance, the Lord will plead the cause of the sinner, execute judgment for him, and vindicate him. The judgment and vindication is executed against the very enemy whom God allowed to rejoice over the sinner.

If the previous statement didn't strike you as amazing or odd or surprising, then we need to pause for an illustration. Let's say that Ricky and Bobby are brothers. Ricky, the older brother, and his buddies are trying to get little Bobby to trespass on old man Roscoe's property. They dare Bobby to sneak over and touch Roscoe's front porch. Ricky tells Bobby that the only sightings of old man Roscoe in the last twenty years has been of his left hand, slightly protruding from his kitchen window while cradling the barrel of a rifle aimed at trespassers. Ricky tells Bobby that he and his buddies all touched the porch as a rite of passage, and if Bobby won't do it, he's chicken and won't be cool. So Bobby, under the pressure of the older boys, plucks up his courage and slithers through the tall grass toward the porch. With his pounding heart threatening the silence of his stealth, Bobby nears the porch, reaches out his hand, and touches the peeling paint.

It's as if a bolt of electricity rushed from his hand up past his shoulder and into his ear lobe. The adrenaline rush yanks him to his feet and he discovers that he's moving rapidly toward safety under the power of his own legs which have taken control of the situation. His churning limbs are a blur of denim as he lunges over the fence and into the thicket where Ricky and his buddies are waiting, sides aching from laughter. "Did you see how big his eyes were?" Ricky guffaws to the neighbor boy. "Look!" says another, "He's still shaking."

It dawns on Bobby that he was deceived and the whole thing was a ruse. They will still call him a chicken and no one thinks he's cool. He bursts into tears. They laugh harder. Now Bobby is running again, this time toward his own porch where he stumbles into his dad's study and tells him the whole story. Father gives Bobby a lecture about trespassing and peer pressure, but the lecture is brief and compassionate because Bobby has already learned his lesson and suffered enough already. At the end of the lecture, father says to Bobby, "Tell your brother I want to speak to him."

Bobby wipes the tears from his eyes. A new confidence begins to grow deep within him. He senses something that suddenly makes him feel a bit taller. That feeling is anticipated vindication. He doesn't know what that means, but he knows that it makes him feel like he's cool. He confidently strides out of the house and up to his brother, who is still grinning and giggling.

Bobby says, "Rejoice not over me, O my enemy! When I fall, I shall rise. When I have dark times, dad will brighten my day. I will accept dad's discipline, because I did something wrong, but then he will come to my aid and justice shall be done. He will take revenge for me." The silly smile begins to leave Ricky's face. Then Bobby adds, "By the way, dad wants to talk to you."

Ashen, Ricky leaves the group and begins the long walk up the driveway. As he opens the storm door, he hears his friends saying, "Good luck, man." Bobby tells them to get off his property, and they leave as if threatened by old man Roscoe himself. Ricky gets a long lecture, with less compassion, and is grounded.

Bobby was guilty of trespassing, goaded by his brother, but dad viewed Ricky's offense as greater, so he vindicated Bobby. In the same way, when we give in to Satan's temptations, we are guilty of sin and suffer those consequences. However, the consequences Satan slaps us with are beyond what God would say is necessary, so He comes to our aid and actually pleads our cause, though we are guilty, and vindicates us!

In a couple places in the New Testament, Paul described some of Satan's activity as teaching and correcting rebellious saints. In 1 Timothy 1:20, Paul names two people whom he had "handed over to Satan to be taught not to blaspheme." Paul actually took the initiative in this woodshed role of Satan.

About the perverse, rebellious man in 1 Corinthians 5:5 who was having an affair with his step mom, Paul said, "Hand this man over to Satan in order to destroy his flesh and to save his spirit." How this works and how one does it is not delineated. Paul seems to be saying that the church should release this man from the spiritual protection of the church so he can suffer the consequences of his behavior. But Paul's purpose was not divine revenge or to prove a point. His ultimate concern was for this man's salvation. Paul reasoned that if Satan got his hands on this guy, the damage would be enough to get his attention and turn him back to God. And we read in 2 Corinthians 2:5-11 that it worked! The fellow repented, and Paul gives instruction on how to lovingly reinstate him. Satan actually helped to bring this man back into healthy relationship with God and the church! (Although that was *not* Satan's intent.)

Sometimes we are too quick to bail people out of their unwise decisions. At those times, we can actually be working against God when we do so. It could be that God is trying to teach them a lesson, and we keep trying to help them out! The *real* way to help them out is to deal with the rebellion first and teach them how to make good choices. If we bail them out without addressing these issues, we are actually enabling their rebellion. This is not true in every troubled life, but often the pain people find themselves in is because they are living out their own choices and not submitting to God's word. There are consequences for that. God allows it to happen. If God won't help them, why would we want to come into conflict with what God is doing? Disobedient saints need discipline from a loving Father. And Father God has set it up so that our disobedient choices, which are in agreement with Satan's plan for us, puts us in Satan's hands to receive the "wage" for our sin (Romans 6:23).

### 3. To strengthen and teach saints.

In 2 Corinthians 12:7-10, Paul describes his thorn in the flesh as a messenger of Satan sent to teach him humility. You can argue whether Paul's thorn was sickness, an eye problem, or his trials described in chapter 11. But these are all just possible *manifestations* of what Paul calls a messenger—literally, an "angel"—of Satan. Paul's thorn was actually some sort of demonic spirit sent by Satan to trouble Paul. Yet the thorn was actually helping Paul, in the sense that it was for his own good. What we would normally think of as an enemy and a bad thing was actually teaching Paul to be humble. What if Paul had become proud and experienced a ministry failure? What would have happened to one-third of the New Testament? It was important that he stay humble, so God allowed a thorn, a messenger of Satan, to make sure Paul stayed humble. The enemy was used for something good.

In a similar fashion, God allowed Satan to attack Job. Although God told Satan he afflicted Job for no reason (Job 2:3), God still had a purpose in the affliction. God was testing and proving Job's faithfulness. And though Job was "blameless and upright" (1:1) he still needed some correction (38:1ff). The trial that Satan brought on Job was used to educate him. The story was preserved as an example to teach us the same lesson. Again, the enemy was used for something good.

It's like death. On this side of eternity, death is public enemy #1. But on the other side of eternity, it will be seen as a friend. Like the little boy in Sunday School who was asked what one needed to do in order to get to heaven. He said, "Die." Death, the enemy, sends us into God's glory! It's weird, when you think about it. But in a similar fashion, Paul's demonic thorn was designed for his benefit.

Paul says in Ephesians 6:12 that we are in a struggle

against unseen forces. It's like a wrestling match. And in any wrestling match, when you struggle, push and pull against your opponent, you get stronger. The same is true in our spiritual struggling against demons. As we resist, rebuke, pray, quote Scripture, worship God, etc, we grow stronger spiritually. One of the exercises a boxer does to prepare for a fight is to hit a punching bag. It strengthens him. There's an illustration of spiritual warfare in that punching bag. Satan and his demons are like a punching bag for us. When we fight against them, we get stronger. God intended it to be that way. Spiritual warfare isn't an unfortunate stroke of a fallen world; it's part of God's plan to strengthen us. By calling the devil a punching bag, I don't mean to diminish his power, mock him or treat his influence flippantly. It's just an illustration. Jude 8-10 warns us not to behave in an arrogant, disrespectful way toward celestial beings we don't fully understand. It's an important warning. So my illustration isn't to ridicule but to make a point.

I should also point out that though the struggle makes us stronger, we aren't in the wrestling match just for the purpose of a spiritual workout. The battle is real, not practice, and we are called to overcome. Paul's description of the struggle as "wrestling" would have brought some images to the minds of a first-century reader. At that time, the loser in a Greek wrestling contest had his eyes gouged out, resulting in blindness for the remainder of his life.[33] In the same way, if we consistently allow demonic spirits to gain the upper hand in our struggle against them, we become blinded spiritually to sin, temptation, and opportunities to do something for God. Our ability to see the spiritual aspects of life is seriously stunted.

David Spooner was youth pastor at a church I served in western Minnesota. He and I once prayed for "Carl," a witch who wanted to renounce his ties to Satanism, witchcraft and other false gods. A number of demons manifested in a variety of ways, but most of them manifested by identifying who they were, using this young man's mouth to speak. Why demons sometimes identify themselves is beyond me. Perhaps they think they can intimidate us by boasting about who they are, what they represent, or what they can do. We weren't impressed. It would seem that demons are more likely to identify themselves when the presence of God is notably strong and they can't help but let the cat out of the bag. I think that was the case in this situation, probably like the demoniacs who would cry out, "You're the Son of God," when they saw Jesus, and He would tell them to pipe down.

As Dave and I prayed for Carl, he began to frantically call out, "I can't see! I can't see!" Then a demon spirit took control of his mouth and said, "I am Spiritual Blindness." Ultimately, one of Satan's goals is to blind us spiritually, either by demonic assignment, as in this case, or other more subtle forms of deception. Proverbs 30:17 says, "The eye that mocks a father, that scorns obedience to a mother, will be pecked out by the ravens of the valley." Ravens were one of those unclean animals in Old Testament times, and in modern times ravens are a favorite of those in witchcraft. Many witches choose to go by the name "Raven." Carl experienced tremendous freedom that night, but regrettably he reverted back to witchcraft and even changed his name to Raven.

It's a battle to be able to see clearly and to ward off spiritual blindness. It's a struggle for us to keep our eyes on Christ, and when we win this struggle, I believe the Enemy receives that blindness back on himself—unable to detect or keep up with what God is doing in our lives. Psalm 69:23 says, "May their eyes be darkened so they cannot see."

You may not be in a battle against the demonic forces of witchcraft like Carl was. But you are in a spiritual battle, whether you realize it or not. The New Testament calls us soldiers; and soldiers are trained to fight. God is a God of the battle. He's a warrior. Anyone who doesn't believe this ought to reread the Old Testament.

But the fight doesn't end when the New Testament begins, and it doesn't end at the cross. The spiritual battle still rages and we are either shooting, being shot at, or caught in the crossfire. You decide your position! Because the battle is spiritual, Paul says in 2 Corinthians 10:3-4 that we shouldn't fight with man-made weapons. Why? Because we aren't fighting men; we're fighting spiritual forces. Those spiritual forces—demons—are left in this world for us to fight against to make us stronger and to make us winners. You can't be a winner until you…umm, win. And you can't win if you don't enter the competition. The competition is against Satan and his demons. That's the role they have in your life. They are not some unfortunate plan B that we got stuck with. They didn't land on earth accidentally when they were kicked out of heaven. God intentionally planned for and placed demons on earth for a purpose. Part of that purpose was to get in our way, the definition of "Adversary," which is the English word for the Hebrew word *satan*. When we push demons out of our way, we get stronger.

Isaiah 54:17 is an encouraging verse: "No weapon forged against you will prevail." That's a great promise for spiritual warfare, but let's put it in context to see more of God's purpose. The context includes a verse we looked at earlier in this chapter:

> "See, it is I who created the blacksmith who fans the coals into flame and forges a weapon fit for its work. And it is I who have created the destroyer to work havoc; no weapon forged against you will prevail, and you will refute every tongue that accuses you. This is the heritage of the servants of the LORD, and this is their vindication from me," declares the LORD.
>
> Isaiah 54:16-17

God created both the blacksmith and the destroyer. The blacksmith makes weapons, but none of those weapons (forged by the blacksmith God created) will prevail against us. And we will refute the accusations of our enemies. The inference is that the destroyer, a "weapon" forged by God to work havoc, will not prevail against us. God created the destroyer to work havoc as an accusing tongue, but this thing God forged will not prevail against us. We can refute its accusations. God created the destroyer and the weapons it uses against us because God means for us to engage in the battle. But He also means for us to win. For us to win, we must first fight. In order to fight, we must have someone to fight against. To have someone to fight against, God created the destroyer.

When the Israelites entered the Promised Land to take possession of it, they could not do so without a fight. God commanded them to drive the evil nations out. However, they were not completely successful in this. There are several reasons for the failure, but one reason that Judges 3:1-2 gives had to do with God's purposes. The text says that God actually left some nations behind to teach warfare to the descendents of those who fought in the battles. God is a God of the battle.

This is not just interesting information; it's also encouraging and exciting. We don't need to be intimidated by any demonic force. The Bible encourages us to fear God, but not to fear anything else. How can we get away with not being afraid? Because we can be assured of victory in this: Demons were placed here *in order to be defeated by Christians, through the power of the Holy Spirit*. The purpose they serve is to be defeated by us.

This mindset changes everything in spiritual warfare, because spiritual warfare is no longer something just for the spiritually elite or the mystics. It's for every Christian, and *every Christian is supposed to win*, because that's the script God wrote. We lose the battle when we forget the script and do it our own way. We lose when we stop fighting. We lose when we think Satan still has some authority and we can't resist his power. But we win when we deny ourselves, take up the cross, follow Jesus, submit to God, and resist the devil. That's the script.

Even Jesus had to submit Himself to the script. Hebrews 4:15 tells us that He was tempted just like we are. We read the details of this temptation in Matthew 4. In verse 1, Matthew explains that the reason Jesus was led *by the Spirit* into the desert was to be tempted by the devil. Have you ever noticed why He was sent into the desert? I used to think it was for a time of solitude, fasting, prayer and communion with the Father before He began His public ministry. The Bible doesn't say that. He was not led into the wilderness to commune with the Father but to be tempted by the devil! He was "led by the Spirit" to interact with the devil! It was part of the plan and Jesus had to go through it like everyone else. Hebrews 5:8 says Jesus learned obedience through suffering, just like the rest of us.

Matthew describes three specific temptations that Satan threw at Jesus. With each one, Jesus responded with Scripture and rejected the influence of the devil. But it wasn't until the third temptation that Jesus told the devil to leave. Why didn't He tell Satan to scram on the first temptation? I believe it was because His time of testing was not complete. Led by the Spirit, Jesus rebuked the devil and commanded Him to leave on the third temptation because He had passed the test and it was time to do ministry. And because spiritual beings do not have a free will, when someone with the authority of God gives them a command, they have no choice but to comply.

The result of Jesus passing this test was increased anointing. Immediately He began to preach with power that the Kingdom of God was near (Matthew 4:17). In the same way, when we pass the test of the wilderness and resist the lie of the Enemy, our effectiveness increases. Also, we are strengthened against further temptations. When the devil left Jesus, the Bible says Satan planned to return when there was another opportunity. That opportunity came when Jesus was crucified. The temptations continued right up until His death, and Jesus resisted each of the devil's temptations. Except this time, the temptations didn't come directly from Satan's mouth. Instead, he had a few willing hosts (people) whom he used as mouthpieces. Each of their temptations while Jesus hung on the cross mirrored the temptations that Jesus went through in the wilderness:

### Temptations of Jesus…

| …in the Wilderness | …on the Cross |
|---|---|
| ➢ "Tell these stones to become bread" | ➢ They offered Him wine |
| ➢ "Throw yourself from the temple so the angels rescue you" | ➢ "You who would destroy and rebuild the temple in three days, come down and we'll believe in You" |
| ➢ "Worship me and I'll give you the world's *kingdoms*" | ➢ "He's the *King* of Israel; let Him save Himself" |

He was able to defeat each temptation on the cross, the most important battle of His life. He was well prepared, having gained experience and strength in the wilderness.

### 4. To prove who is true and who is false.

The testing that Satan imposes on us is not just for us to gain strength and experience. Sadly, some do not pass the test. Sometimes I wish the testing wasn't so severe, because it causes some fence riders to fall away. But if the fence riders stayed in the fold and weren't tested, the result would be insincere, phony Christians.

In Luke 22:31 on the eve of the crucifixion, Jesus told Peter that Satan had asked to test the disciples. "Simon, Simon," He said, "Satan has asked to sift you as wheat." We might think Jesus was speaking only of Simon's testing, but the word "you" is plural in Greek. The testing was for *all* the disciples.[34] This testing was compared to the sifting of wheat. When wheat is sifted, the wheat is separated from the husk—the good separated from the bad.[35] And that is, of course, exactly what happened. Judas (a "husk") was separated from the others. Satan asked, and was given permission, to sift. Judas got sifted.

In chapter five, we examined Revelation 12 and saw that Satan no longer gets an audience with God to ask permission to sift us. Now, he tries to do it without permission. But there is a big difference between what is available now versus what was available to the Twelve when they were sifted. We are on the other side of the cross, the other side of the Resurrection, and the other side of Pentecost. The blood of Jesus has been shed, Christ rose from the dead, and the Holy Spirit dwells within true disciples of Jesus.

So, Christian, be both warned and encouraged: Satan will test you in an attempt to see if you are genuine or not. Don't fail this test and don't lose the battle. Make sure you are trusting only in the death and resurrection of Jesus to save you. And make sure you are not trusting in your own strength to pass the test but in the power of the Holy Spirit—the same Spirit that raised Jesus from the dead.

## 5.  To accent God's holiness.

We have already discussed the comparison of good and evil with dark and light or hot and cold. Have you ever noticed how much you appreciate heat in your home (for those who live in climates that are less than mild) when you come in from the cold? And have you ever noticed how little effect a flashlight has on a sunny day? Yet that same flashlight seems so bright at night. In the same way, having demons around makes God look that much better. Forgiveness is so sweet to the sinner. Healing is only useful for the sick. Holiness looks so beautiful against Satan's ugliness.

## 6. To provide humans a choice.

God could have made us righteous robots. History wouldn't be very interesting, though. God already had a choice-free environment in heaven (assuming that the angels cannot rebel, as discussed earlier). What He wanted from mankind was a race that followed Him sacrificially, as a choice of their will, not as a result of their programming. In order to have a legitimate choice, there had to be a tempter—an enticer, a choice-suggester—to offer an alternative to God's perfect plan. Satan did that through the serpent in the Garden, and humans have been regularly choosing Satan's plan ever since.

Yet there is a minority of human beings, growing and gaining strength, who choose to reject the perverted counterfeit that Satan imposes and instead choose to follow the teachings of Jesus Christ. That's powerful and beautiful. I'm inspired by people who doggedly follow Jesus in the midst of trial and temptation. None of that inspiration would have been possible without Satan. He serves a purpose in God's design.

# CHAPTER EIGHT
# AUTHORITY IN SPIRITUAL WARFARE

W e often talk about how Satan is a "defeated foe." Yet something about that idea has never satisfied me. If he's defeated, why are we still fighting him? Some explain this by describing our situation as being like the time between D-Day and V-Day in World War II—the time between the days in which the war was decided and the fighting actually stopped. Fighting continued in between because it took time to get the word out that victory had been determined.

There is merit to that illustration in that Satan is defeated yet we still fight. But it's not completely satisfying, either, because Satan and his demons know exactly what happened on the cross. They know they were out-smarted and that the blood of Jesus was and is powerful not only for the forgiveness of sins, but for deliverance and freedom from the power of sin. They know this and continue to fight, but not because they are unaware of their defeat. They continue to do battle, I believe, because of the purpose for which they were created, as we saw in the last chapter.

It is true that Satan is a defeated foe, in the sense that Jesus thoroughly defeated him to the point of humiliation (Colossians 2:15). Satan lost to Jesus, but he has not lost to the church. Yet.

1 John 3:8 says Jesus came into the word to destroy the works of the devil, and we being Christ's body ought to continue in that work of destroying the kingdom of darkness. We are charged to defeat Satan in our lives according to the example that Jesus set for us.

Colossians 2:15 says Jesus disarmed Satan. He disarmed him in the sense that Satan's authority to wield death was forfeited to Jesus, who now holds the keys to death and Hades (Revelation 1:18). However, there is still one weapon that Satan retains: the lie. If he can get us to believe an idea that is false and we live according to that belief, he's got us. It's as if he did something bad to us, but in truth we did it to ourselves by being taken by his deceptive persuasion.

Like darts, his lies are hurled at us in two forms: temptation and accusation. When Satan tempts us, he's saying, "Try this. You'll like it. It's OK. God wants you to be happy. It's a good thing and God wouldn't want to withhold something you would want. It's really not all that bad." His enticements are all lies. But when we give in to it, he comes back to say, "You *did* it! You're guilty! You don't deserve to be called a Christian." There may be a little truth mixed with his lies, but only enough to provide the deception needed to fuel the lies. It's ironic that he would accuse of us things we did at his suggestion, but that's exactly what he does. And even if we don't yield to his temptations, he will still accuse us anyway, of things we *didn't* do: "You *thought* about it, you perverted hypocrite!" In the case of Job, Satan still accused Job even though the man was what we would call "above reproach." Essentially, Satan accused Job of goodness based on bribery. That is, he accused Job of being good only because God blessed him so much.

But these charges were dismissed through a *trial*. Remember from chapter five the discussion about Revelation 12 where we talked about Satan being the prosecuting attorney and Jesus being the defense attorney? Do you get the courtroom picture? Job was under *trial*. The charges were dismissed. He passed the test. God was glorified. Job was strengthened. Satan's lies were exposed.

A lot of spiritual warfare is just that: exposing Satan's lies and deception and replacing them with Truth. Remember, Satan does not hold the weapon of death anymore. Jesus holds the keys. Satan cannot directly kill, but he can accomplish destruction *indirectly* by getting people to believe his lies. He can't push us off the cliff, but he can suggest that we jump. "It will be exciting," he says. "Think of the rush on the way down! And at the bottom, a lovely cushion of feathers to alight upon."

His lies are meant to entice us to make decisions that will cause in our lives what he does not have the right to do to us himself. So he tells us lies about God: "God isn't really good, so you can't trust Him. You better take matters into your own hands. He doesn't really love you. He loves others, but not you—you're too dirty." And he tells us lies about ourselves: "You can't be forgiven for what you've done. You're unworthy and hopeless. You might as well give up." Neil Anderson has aptly pointed out that freedom is impossible unless we see the truth about who God is and who we are in light of the cross. We are God's children. And if we believe that, we'll begin to behave like it. That behavior is called "freedom."[36]

But in addition to the lies Satan tries to tell us about God and ourselves, there is a third type of lie he peddles. Satan tells us lies about himself. Primarily, he tries to convince Christians that he doesn't really exist. Barna Research Group discovered in a 1999 study that 45% of people claiming to be born again Christians deny Satan's existence. The study found that 70% of Catholics, 62% of Protestant mainline church attendees, 49% of Protestant non-mainline church attendees, and 43% of

Baptists believe the devil is non-existent—that Satan is only a symbol of evil.[37]

The *truth* is, you simply cannot call yourself a Bible-believing Christian and not believe that the devil is a real, spiritual *person*. If we categorize references to Satan in Scripture as the personification of evil, where does the allegorizing stop? Is the Holy Spirit, or God for that matter, the personification of good? If we say we believe the Bible, we cannot help but recognize that there is a spiritual person called Satan.

The problem is, too many Christians don't read the Bible consistently. Too many are unfamiliar with what the Bible says, and not enough have allowed its truth to shape their thinking, beliefs, and doctrines. Satan has seized that opportunity and convinced them he isn't real. If he can convince us that he doesn't exist, then we won't fight against him. And he would prefer that we didn't fight back!

If he can't convince us that he doesn't exist, he will push other lies about himself. He will suggest to us that demonic activity only took place during New Testament times or that it takes place now only in Africa or some other far off place—the belief that described my life as a "Christian Sadducee." Or, he'll convince us that because we've prayed the sinner's prayer, we're immune to demonic influence, so any sin-habits or unresolved spiritual conflicts we struggle with are essentially the result of our upbringing, personality, lack of will power, etc.

Another place of deception I believe the church has bought into is the whole Lucifer story. When we believe that Satan was a good angel gone bad, and that he tried to overthrow God and now he tries to damage God's Kingdom by deceiving people, it puts us on the defensive. But if we understand that Satan was created as he is for the specific purposes we've been discussing here (see chapter seven), then we realize that we can and should be on the *offensive*. It's no longer about us trying to protect and preserve what God has given us and "holding the fort till Jesus comes." Instead, *we* are on the offensive, understanding that Satan must give up the ground we are taking back—ground he has usurped. If we understand that God *planned* that we be in a struggle against Satan, and if we believe that God is truly good and perfect and wants the best for His children, then we will not only be motivated to fight, but we'll have the faith to win.

God not only planned for us to fight Satan, He planned for us to win! That knowledge strengthens our faith. And winning this fight is a matter of faith. What you believe determines what you do and how you will live. If you don't believe you can defeat Satan through the power of Jesus, you probably won't. But if you confidently

> God *planned* for us to fight Satan. And He planned for us to *win*.

take up the shield of faith and the sword of the Spirit (the word of God) and resist the devil, he will flee—something a *scared* person does. What helps to have that confidence? A proper understanding of who God is, who you are in light of God's love, and who the Enemy is and what God's purpose is for us in relation to that Enemy.

These are the important tools (or weapons) you need in your tool chest (or arsenal) to defeat Satan:
1.  The Word of God
2.  Prayer (and fasting)
3.  Faith
4.  Authority

These are discussed below.

## 1. The Word of God

When tempted three times by Satan, Jesus answered three times with Scripture. It's not just that it's powerful against the enemy, the word of God also tunes our minds toward truth. We cannot hope to beat the devil if we are confused. We are instructed to "gird up the loins of our minds" (1 Peter 1:13). In other words, *be alert and think clearly*, and take every thought captive (2 Corinthians 10:5). How do we capture a thought? By surrounding it with *truth*. Romans 10:17 says faith, another necessary weapon discussed below, comes by *hearing*, and hearing comes through the message of Christ. The word of God (especially the words of Jesus) feeds our faith; and faith strengthens us for the battle.

If you don't have a regular diet of Bible reading (that means daily), then I'd have to wonder why you're reading this book. Do you really think this book will better equip you for spiritual warfare than the Bible would? We simply cannot expect to be strong and healthy spiritually if we're starving. And the Word of God is where we begin to feed our spirit. Deuteronomy 8:3 makes a connection between manna and the word of God. Jesus made a similar connection in John 6. God's provision of manna to the Israelites is a great illustration of the role of the Bible in our lives. Think of these qualities about manna (from Exodus 16:1-5, 13-21):

1. Manna was a miracle gift of God's provision.
2. Manna was nourishing (when eaten!).
3. Manna came daily (not weekly, monthly or yearly).
4. It had to be gathered. In fact, it was *work* to be gathered. Each family gathered for themselves. Moses didn't deliver it; but he gave instructions about how to get it.

These same attributes apply to the nourishment the Bible gives our spirit:

1. The Bible is a miracle gift of God's provision.
2. The Bible is nourishing to our soul and spirit (but only when read, believed and obeyed).

3. The Bible is to be taken daily (not weekly, monthly or yearly!). Did you know that if you spend just fifteen minutes a day reading the Bible you can read through the entire Bible in one year? Give up one thirty-minute TV program a day and you can read through the Bible *twice* in one year!

4. The Bible must be "gathered." In fact, it's *work* to be gathered. Each person must gather for himself, not be spoon-fed by the pastor. Your pastor's job is to give you instructions about how to read and understand it. But as you mature, you need to feed yourself. A shepherd (pastor) leads the sheep to the grass and the sheep graze. The shepherd doesn't pull up the blades of grass so the sheep can eat from his hand.

I have talked to people who have "already read" the Bible so they see no need to read it again (as if they remember everything in it!). Yet these same people have eaten hamburgers hundreds of times in their lives. Why? Not because they didn't know what the hamburger tasted like. That's the whole point! They *did* know what it tasted like, so they wanted another! If we know what the Bible says, and we enjoy that, why wouldn't we want to read it again? Especially if we're hungry. Proverbs 27:7 says, "He who is full loathes honey, but to the hungry even what is bitter tastes sweet." Are we hungry for the word of God? If so, it will taste good to our souls.

As a pastor, I am concerned that so many Christians know so little about the Bible and so few take the time to read it daily. We are a lot like the Israelites, who took the manna for granted. Numbers 11 tells us they got tired of it and craved meat instead. Can you imagine? I mean, I like a juicy steak as much as the next guy, but can you believe that they would take this miracle meal—this bread from heaven—for granted? Wouldn't you have liked to have tasted manna? But the Israelites complained that they didn't have anything to eat and they had no appetite!

So they demanded the *flesh* of animals to eat.

Are you seeing the comparison? We must be careful to appreciate the gift that the Bible is to us. Let's not take it for granted, get tired of it, lose our appetite for it, and then demand "flesh." God gave the Israelites the flesh they wanted. He gave them so much it made them sick! The same thing can happen to us. If we want our flesh more than His Word, He will let us have it. But it will make us sick.

In John 14:15, Jesus said, "If you love me, you will obey what I command." If we say that we love Jesus, we will not only love to read, we'll love to obey His Word. Think about it. If you love someone, you want to hear what he says. You can tell if someone loves you, because she'll listen to you, even if what you're saying isn't interesting. She'll even laugh at all your stupid jokes. It's not so different with God. He loves you, so He listens to your prayer requests. Even your pathetic ones! So on the flip side, if we love Him, then we will want to hear what *He* has to say. His Word will take on new interest for us.

Reading the Bible is absolutely essential for spiritual growth and success in spiritual warfare. Contrary to what people may subconsciously think, spiritual maturity is not instantaneous, automatic, or mystical. We aren't instantly mature when we believe in Jesus. We have to grow and growth comes from being fed. Growth in Christ is not automatic, just because we show up at church. Just like a student can go to school and not learn anything, a Christian must apply himself to the Bible to get anything out of it. This growth is not mystical, as if you could put the Bible under your pillow and its truth and power seeps into your brain and spirit while you sleep. If we expect to grow spiritually, we're going to have to work at it. We must be students of God's Word. Now, we can't make ourselves grow. Only God can make something grow. But just like a farmer who tills, waters and fertilizes his crop, we work the soil of our hearts with God's Word and God produces growth in us.[38]

Psalm 1:2 says the successful man is one who both delights and meditates on God's Word day and night. In other words, he doesn't just read it; he thinks (meditates) about it. And he doesn't just study it; he actually enjoys (delights in) it! So I'm not talking about gritting your teeth, plowing through a few verses each day then saying, "There. I survived it." The picture in Psalm 1 is that of enjoying the Bible. How do you enjoy it? The more you read and meditate on it, the more enjoyable it becomes, but the real enjoyment comes when you actually believe what it says and you obey its instructions. In fact, it's impossible not to obey it if you truly believe it. Your obedience is evidence that you believe. When you begin to see the positive effects of God's Word in your life, it gets more enjoyable.

John 8:32 says the truth is what sets us free. In this book on spiritual warfare, nothing can be more critical to your victory than appreciating and applying God's Word in your life. Daily Bible reading, regular Bible study, consistent meditation and even Bible memorization are all *necessary* disciplines to arm us in the battle against Satan. Without them, you might as well set this book aside. Nothing I can say here will help you. All I'm doing in this book is expounding on the Word of God and pointing out its truth to you so you can apply it to your life more effectively. The foundation is God's truth, revealed in the Bible. Without that foundation, this book has nothing to build on.

## 2. Prayer (and fasting)

The time for prayer is not when confronting a demon. Jesus and the apostles never stopped to pray when confronted by a demonized person. Instead, they commanded the spirit to leave. They had already done their praying. Jesus often withdrew from the people to find a solitary place to pray. His hours in prayer strengthened Him with power and authority so that when the time came, He could function in that power and authority.

The apostles learned this. In the opening chapters of the book of Acts the apostles were always on their way from, on their way to, or in a prayer meeting. So when they bumped into the demonized, they *healed* them. They didn't even pray for them! We must be people of prayer *before* we attempt to release someone from demonic bondage. And fasting is an important aspect of that. It weakens demons and it weakens the influence of the flesh in your life. When you fast, you are informing your flesh—your natural appetites that want to control you—that it is not in charge. Demons need compliant flesh to work with, so when you fast you remove opportunities for them to exploit you since you are subduing your flesh. At one point, Jesus cast out a demon the disciples couldn't handle, because He had spent time in prayer and fasting that the disciples hadn't spent (Mark 9:29).

## 3. Faith

I'm a little nervous taking on this topic because there's been so much written with so many different opinions about the role of faith in releasing miracles and God's power. One opinion says if we have faith, then any miracle is available to us when we believe and confess it. This view can certainly be supported by verses in the Bible. For example, Matthew 9:22 says, "Your faith has healed you." And Matthew 21:22 says, "If you believe, you will receive whatever you ask for in prayer."

But is that the whole story? Some would say it isn't the whole story; there are examples in Scripture when good, faithful men of God did *not* get their prayer answered. It's an intense debate that I joined in the past, but refuse to do so now. Though both sides have valid points, both sides can lead to misuses of Scripture.

For example, how is it helpful for me to tell someone who is sick that if he just believes harder or finds something to repent of, he will be healed? Many people have given this advice to sick people who have remained sick. And when they remain sick, that counsel adds guilt and unnecessary self-analysis to their illness. The self-analysis often detracts from focusing on Jesus and whatever miracle-working faith they might have had is drowned in the doubt of self-consciousness.

On the other hand, how consoling is it to "encourage" a sick person when we share Scriptural examples of other people who didn't get healed? We don't want them to feel guilty for lacking faith or something, so we tell them, "See, you're not the only one! Look at these sick people in the Bible." And they think, *Great. So I'm not the only one. Thanks. But I'm still SICK!* I'm sure there's a measure of validity with both of these viewpoints, but either side runs the risk of trying to subject God to a personal doctrinal preference. Neither side should attempt to interpret the Bible based on the results of their prayers or what fits their personalities and desires.

So at the risk of sounding like a fence-rider, I'm going to sidestep that issue and avoid discussing how and when faith works. Instead, I want to discuss what faith *is* and how we get it. Faith does work. The Bible clearly teaches that. So we need to make sure we have it—true faith—because when we have it the Bible helps us understand how it works and the Holy Spirit helps us know how to use it. Perhaps one of the reasons why the debate over faith has raged is because we haven't correctly defined faith or looked at other elements besides faith in working miracles.

So I'd like to try to put faith in its proper place with other tools and weapons of kingdom advancement. What I mean to say is that faith alone does not appear to be enough for doing spiritual warfare. Before you throw stones at me, I'm not talking about doing good works in addition to faith in order to get something from God. The missing element in our spiritual warfare is not good works; it's *authority*. Authority is an important means to exercise faith.

In Matthew 10:1, Jesus gave the disciples *authority*, not faith, to drive out unclean spirits. Authority will be discussed next, under #4, but I mention it here simply to point out that telling someone their problem is "lack of faith" ignores other factors in spiritual warfare and treats faith as some sort of genie. We must not make an idol out of faith or put our faith in our faith—that is, we should not put our trust in our ability to believe.

> Jesus gave the disciples *authority*, not just *faith*, to drive out unclean spirits.

When our prayers aren't answered the way we expect, we often feel like we need more faith to get our prayers answered. The disciples felt the same way and asked Jesus for more faith. But He responded by telling them they didn't need more faith as long as they had a teensy-weensy amount of faith. (The theological term is "mustard seed"—Matthew 17:20).

Speaking of believing, when it comes to miracles and victory over Satan we should recognize a distinction between belief and faith. Believing God will do what we ask is closely tied to hope. This hopeful belief could be rooted in faith, but it could also be rooted simply in our deep desire to see God do what we want. But simply wanting God to do something may have nothing to do with God's plans for us. We must be careful not to base our faith on what we want or what we think God should do. That's presumption, not faith. Nor should we base our faith on how hard we believe.

For example, statements like, "I really, really believe God will do this; there is no doubt in my mind that He'll do this;

I know just because I know," may not be a "word of faith" at all. It may be a word of hope, confidence, belief or wishful thinking. Believing something will happen because you *want* it to happen or because you think it *should* happen is not good enough. It may be belief, but it's not necessarily faith.

Trying to change the world through the power of your belief is actually a New Age concept.[39] It's positive thinking, not faith. True faith is based on God's Word and God's purpose. God's miracles always align with His will and purpose, and we must be acquainted with His Word to discern His will, His ways, and His purpose. Romans 10:17 says faith comes by hearing the Word. In other words, when you read the Bible, faith comes. The Christian who says, "I believe God will answer my prayer," but hasn't read his Bible in weeks, can't tell you where the book of Obadiah is, and looks in the table of contents when you tell him to turn to Hezekiah chapter two, has no right to suggest what God will do. He's using God for his own desires and isn't really in decent fellowship with Jesus. It's not faith. It may be belief and it may be sincere, but it's a belief based on his own definition of God and what that god should do. Faith resides in the spirit and is fed by the Scriptures and released into us by the Holy Spirit. Belief resides in the mind and can be based on a number of things, including mind-games we play with ourselves.

You may have heard of George Müller who established and ran orphanages in England in the 1800s. Mr. Müller's orphanages were funded completely by faith. He never requested provision from anyone—except God. Imagine that: a ministry that never received an offering, asked for money, or did fundraisers. All he did was pray for God to provide, and God would respond. My favorite story is the time George Müller sat down with the children for breakfast. The only problem was that there was no food. Mr. Müller simply bowed his head and asked for God's provision.

At that moment, a milk truck and an egg truck collided outside the orphanage. During that time in history, a "truck" was a horse-drawn carriage and there were no refrigerated vehicles. Drivers needed to deliver food quickly before it spoiled. So when these two wagons collided, they were both rendered inoperable and something needed to be done with the food immediately. As Mr. Müller said "amen" to his prayer for breakfast, there was a knock at the door. The two drivers asked him if he had any need of milk and eggs. George Müller thanked God and they had breakfast!

We hear stories like that and we classify George Müller as a man of faith and prayer. And that would not be inaccurate. But what you may not know, even if you have heard of George Müller, is that he was also a man of the Word. His practice was to read through the entire Bible, not once or twice a year, but *four times per year*. That's about thirteen chapters every day.

I once read through the Bible twice in one year. It seemed overwhelming to me at times. Miss one day and I was seven chapters behind. Now in George Müller's case, he didn't just read his chapters and go his way, he labored over each passage in prayer. No wonder he had such faith! No wonder his prayers had such impact! He was a man of the Word. He knew how to pray because he knew how God thought. He learned that through God's Word. And yes, he had faith. But I believe his faith was the result of his time in the Word, because *faith comes by hearing God's Word.*

Faith is not just believing. 1 Corinthians 12 identifies faith as a manifestation of the Spirit. Miracle-working faith is not something we can conjure up in our minds through mental calisthenics. It is released by

> Faith is the personality of Jesus resident in what our souls hope for.

the Spirit in us for God's purposes and glory. Hebrews 11 defines faith as "being sure" (NIV) of what we hope for. "Being sure" is what the KJV calls "substance." It's a tricky word to translate into English. It could actually be translated as "person" or "being" (as in Hebrews 1:3). In other words, *faith is the personality of Jesus resident in what our souls hope for.* It comes from the Holy Spirit, revealed in God's Word. It's not just a mental belief; it's a miraculous confidence that faces impossible odds without fear. The equation below shows the relationship between faith and belief:

## FAITH = BELIEF + TRUST

Most people think belief and faith are synonymous. But you can believe something based on positive thinking, then throw in the Name of Jesus and think you have faith. But if it's not fed by God's Word and inspired by the Holy Spirit, it is only belief. Miracle-working faith does not just believe. It also trusts when the miracle doesn't come in the time or way that was asked for. Belief says, "I know God will do this." Trust says, "But even if He doesn't, His ways are best." Both of these attitudes are necessary if it's real faith. Remember the three Hebrew men thrown into the fiery furnace? They had great confidence (faith) that God would rescue them. They *believed* God could rescue them, but they were still ready to *trust* Him if He didn't. They said, "If we are thrown into the blazing furnace, the God we serve is able to save us from it, and he will rescue us from your hand, O King. *But even if he does not*, we want you to know, O king, that we will not serve your gods or worship the image of gold you have set up" (Daniel 3:17-18, emphasis added).

If your faith does not remain intact when God *doesn't* answer your prayer, you don't have miracle-working, Biblical faith. Biblical faith *trusts* God anyway, even when things don't go as expected. When facing the Enemy, *that's* the kind of faith you need, not some drummed up, positive-thinking belief system dangled in front of you by a TV preacher with a four-button suit and expensive jewelry.

## 4. Authority

There is a significant misunderstanding in the area of the authority the believer has in spiritual warfare. It's important that we develop doctrine based on Scripture and not pop theology, so let's compare common thought with Biblical truth.

There is a cliché that has been going around for who knows how long about spiritual warfare that says we need to "take authority" over the devil. But as we saw from the discussion about Revelation 12 in chapter five, authority is never *taken* (according to God's Word); it is always *given*. So we can't literally "take authority." I think I know what people mean when they say, "I take authority over the devil." What they mean is that they are *exercising the authority Christ has given them.*

You might think I'm splitting hairs about this and just playing with words, but there's more to it than that. The problem arises when people who *don't* have that authority try to *take* it and attempt to slap demons around. The outcome? They are ineffective and become disillusioned in the process, thinking that spiritual warfare doesn't work. Or, they yell at demons, convince themselves they've done something wonderful (when nothing actually happened), then ignore the glaring reality that nothing has changed. Worse yet, as in the case of the sons of Sceva in Acts 19, they get hurt (or hurt someone else) in the process. You may argue that the sons of Sceva weren't really born again so they didn't possess any authority. However, the Bible does not teach that being born again means we immediately and automatically have authority over evil spirits.

It's a commonly held belief, but it's an assumption without any sound Scriptural backing. Let's talk about how and when we receive authority.

Authority was originally given to humanity when God gave Adam dominion over the earth. Adam forfeited dominion to Satan, who possessed that authority until he yielded it to Jesus at the cross. Remember, authority is always given. It's never taken. We can be tricked into trading it away, but it can never be stolen from us. We can't take authority from Satan, because he doesn't have it anymore. At the death and resurrection of Jesus, all authority was given to Jesus. Satan no longer possessed the authority he tricked Adam into giving him. We can't take authority from God, because God doesn't work that way. He *gives* to His children. We are not allowed, nor are we able, to take anything from Him.

All authority was given to Jesus so He now has the right to share it with whomever He wills. And with whom does He share it? Many of us were taught that when we pray the "sinner's prayer" we instantly have access to the riches and powers of heaven. The Bible doesn't teach that. In fact, the Bible doesn't teach anything about a "sinner's prayer."

A theology of salvation has been developed (probably from sharing the Gospel with children) in which we tell people to ask Jesus into their hearts and to do so we teach them to pray the sinner's prayer. Here's a shocker: you won't find a sinner's prayer in the Bible nor will you find anyone asking Jesus into his heart. I'm not saying those are bad concepts, just incomplete concepts. They are so incomplete that if asking Jesus into one's heart with the sinner's prayer is the main directive when leading someone to Jesus, we have left out so much of the story that we have probably misled them into a false conversion experience.

The Bible describes our role in receiving salvation as a radical decision of repentance and faith, followed by a life of intense obedience and commitment. The work of the Holy Spirit in convicting of sin and regenerating our spirits are necessary elements of a true salvation experience. The Biblical understanding of conversion was an experience that followed repentance. Biblical Christians were committed to living a holy life in order to avoid the wrath of God directed at sinful behavior. New Testament believers were in awe of the sacrifice of Christ and they were willing to sacrifice their lives in return, if necessary. But modern evangelism tends to focus on how Jesus can meet our needs and make us happy. Sinners are encouraged to jump on board for the promised benefits, often without being instructed in sacrifice, obedience, and commitment. They are told to invite Jesus into their lives through the sinner's prayer without being told they also need to *give their lives to* Jesus. It is right to invite Jesus into one's life, but it's an incomplete understanding of conversion. And if information is left out of a story such that the listener is led to believe something contrary to the truth, then the story is false, even if the portion that *was* presented is accurate.

Modern evangelism tends to put an unbiblical emphasis on Jesus as Savior with little mention or discussion of Jesus as Lord. But the New Testament's description of Jesus is the opposite. For every reference to Jesus being Savior, there are at least seventeen references to Jesus being Lord. In the New Testament, God is called "Lord" twenty to twenty-four times more than He is called Savior (depending on your interpretation). In fact, the word "savior" only appears twenty-four times in the entire New Testament, whereas the word "Lord," when used to reference God or Jesus, is used well over 500 times.

However, much of modern evangelism focuses only on Jesus saving us, forgetting that this Savior, as *Lord*, requires obedience through a life of holiness. Since holiness is not a popular message and we want to see people saved and churches grow, modern evangelism has often taken the Gospel from a call-to-commitment and reduced it to a sales pitch. This modern gospel offers life-improvement, but the true Gospel calls us to lay down our life. The true Gospel creates servants of Jesus Christ. The modern Gospel creates clients and customers of Jesus Christ. The focus of today's Gospel is primarily on what God does for *me*, being careful not to impose on our lifestyle by asking us to do something for *God*.

Lest I am misunderstood, I should point out that I am not talking about legalism. Legalism is an attempt to please God through our own efforts or to earn something (like salvation) from Him. Legalism nullifies grace and compromises the salvation message. It tends to feed off of fear, judgment, and externals and it sacrifices relationship with Jesus for the sake of performance.

Paul identified legalistic doctrines as having demonic origins (1 Timothy 4:1, 3). Rather, I am talking about obedience and commitment to righteousness that is not based on "have to" but "want to." I am talking about living out a desire to please the Lord, through a holy life, because of a love for Jesus. It's not based on fear, punishment or merit, it's based on love, worship and commitment.

I'm spending a lot of time on this, not just because the doctrine of salvation is central to the Gospel, but because it has significance with our understanding about the availability of authority. If people come to Jesus to improve their life instead of getting right with God, the natural assumption is, as children of the King, that possessing tremendous authority is instant and automatic with conversion. People believe and act as if such authority is their *right* as God's children, when really it is a privilege that comes with great responsibility.

What the Bible teaches is that Jesus gives authority to those with whom He has close relationship. In Mark 3:14-15 Jesus "appointed twelve—designating them apostles—that they might be with him and that he might send them out to preach and to have authority to drive out demons." The authority to drive out demons is accompanied with, or perhaps followed by, *being with Him*. So they did that, the first job of the apostle: to be with Jesus. His disciples began following Him in Matthew 4, but it wasn't until Matthew 10 that He gave them authority. He didn't give them authority the minute they put down the fishing nets and began to follow. They followed Him for a time *before* He gave them authority. The authority came later, as they grew in their faith. And it continued to grow, with a significant boost on the day of Pentecost. We must realize that we are not instantly given authority over all demonic forces the moment we are saved. Rather, as we grow in our relationship to Jesus, He gives us authority.

Authority is the *authorization* to use power. Take, for instance, the keys to the car. The first time a parent hands the keys to his son is not when the boy is born. He has to grow a bit before he can see over the steering wheel. Turning sixteen doesn't automatically mean he gets the keys either. He has to prove himself faithful in lesser things. If the kid ends up in the river every time he goes for a bike ride, dad will be slow to give him the keys to the car. If he's irresponsible about chores around the house, what's to make dad think Junior will suddenly become responsible behind the wheel? In the same way, why do Christians think they have the right (authority) to rebuke demons when they haven't proven themselves faithful (responsible) in other areas of their lives? Christians who aren't in the Word, have no prayer life, don't tithe, and view church attendance as optional or at least negotiable, should stay out of the demon-rebuking business because it would be like a six year old trying to drive a Hummer. Dangerous.

For example, give an immature Christian the authority to

raise the dead, and he might go out and empty all the cemeteries. It would be mayhem! The Scriptural example is that Jesus shares His authority with those He has close relationship. In that relationship there is a proving or development period.

Christians who are not disciplined spiritually or aren't in touch with Jesus really don't have much authority, despite what their belief tells them (they think that belief is "faith"). They've watched enough evangelists on TV so they figure they know how it's done. So, like the virtual apostles on cable, they try to *take* authority over spirits. But this is not how the disciples functioned. They never had to *take* authority over demons, because they had already been *given* authority. Once authority was given to them, they just functioned in that authority. They didn't have to tell demons they were "taking authority" over them. They just gave the command (e.g., Acts 16:18) and the demons had to comply because the disciples had authority. Biblical examples show disciplined Christians in close friendship to their Lord simply functioning in the authority they were given through their relationship with Jesus.

In the context of that relationship, authority is imparted through the *command* of Christ. In John 10:18, Jesus was explaining that no one could take His life from Him, but that He would lay it down of His own accord. He called that privilege "authority," and explained how He acquired it:

> "No one takes [my life] from me, but I lay it
> down of my own accord. I have authority to
> lay it down and authority to take it up again.
> This command I received from my Father."

The word "command" is unexpected. We might have expected Him to say, "I have authority to lay it down and authority to take it up again. This *authority* I received from my Father." Or maybe, "…This *right*, or *privilege*, or *power*, I received from my Father." But Jesus says, "I have authority, and this *command* I received from my Father," making "authority" and "command" sound almost synonymous. Since His authority was received via command, perhaps a better English word than *command* in John 10:18 would be "mandate." A mandate is an order, like a command, but a mandate carries with it the ability or power to carry out that order. A mandate includes *empowerment*.

If your boss ordered you to flap your arms and fly from Minneapolis to Houston, it would be a frustrating and impossible assignment. But if he handed you a plane ticket and told you to fly to Houston, it has the potential of being an enjoyable experience as you ride the power of the jet engines. His request becomes more than just an order; it's now a mandate, because he provided the means to accomplish the order when he gave it to you.

In the "Great Commission" (Matthew 28:18-19), Jesus told the disciples that all authority had been given to Him, then He gave the *command* to go and disciple the nations. If we don't understand that authority is given through command, we might misinterpret Jesus' words in this way: "All authority has been given to me; therefore I have the right to tell you what to do. So *go!*" But this is *not* what Jesus was saying. He was not just giving them an order to go and disciple, He was giving them a mandate—a command with built-in power. The power He gave was authority, just like the Father had given Him. He passed it on to the disciples via the command "go."

Not only is authority received through a command, authority is also utilized by command. Authority is exercised over demons by commanding them to leave, come out, let go, etc (Acts 16:18, for example). In Mark 1:27, the Jews were amazed at the power Jesus had over demons. They said, "A new teaching—and with authority! He even gives orders to evil spirits and they obey him." Demons *must* obey a command given in authority of the Name of Jesus.

Authority is given by command. When we obey an authoritative command, we walk in the authority of that command. And when *we* give the command to demons, *they* must obey because of the authority given to us.

So what happens to the Christian who tries to take authority he doesn't have? What he's actually taking is *control*, or *trying* to take control. Control is a man-made substitute for God-given authority. Control is something we try to take. Taking control is the attempt to manipulate people or circumstances *or demons* so that a situation becomes more favorable. We all know the annoying person who always tries to take control. It's not you, of course, it's always that other guy! But taking control or taking charge is not what we are called to. It's authority we need, not control. The result of trying to take control is that we attempt to accomplish with the flesh (our personality, natural abilities, charm, intelligence, money or whatever) what can only be accomplished through the power of the Spirit.

There is only one thing that Scripture gives us permission to control, and that thing is *ourselves*. Self-control is a fruit of the Spirit (Galatians 5:23). We are not given permission to control anyone or anything else. Not

> *Control* is a man-made substitute for God-given *authority*. We "take control." God *gives* authority.

even demons. Trying to control demons or do spiritual warfare in the strength or wisdom of the flesh puts us on shaky ground. Not only are we bound for a beating of some sort, like the sons of Sceva, we are also guilty of another offense: witchcraft and divination.

What do I mean by that? I mean that attempts to manipulate

spiritual forces through the power of the mind, mouth or other human efforts are what New Age is all about. Attempting to control demons is exactly what channellers, spiritists, Wiccans, witches, and Satanists attempt to do. Attempting to control spirits is not Scriptural, *even if done in the Name of Jesus*, as Sceva's sons attempted.

Remember, *control* is the attempt to manipulate situations to make them more favorable. But *authority* is the channel for God's power to transform difficult circumstances into God-glorifying miracles. Without that authority, attempts to control demonic interference by shouting, rebuking or conversing with spirits is little different than a witch, soothsayer, or channeller invoking spirits with some incantation. Let's be careful in our interaction with the spirit-world, and do so only in a Biblical, Spirit-led fashion. By exercising authority in Jesus, we aren't trying to control demons, we are *expelling* them and *defeating* their work for the glory of God.

Seeing how important authority is, how can we ensure that we have it? How do we get it? Since authority is *given*, not taken or earned, it is a gift. We can't force it or presume it. But there are some things we can do to prepare our hearts to receive it:

1.  *Get close to Jesus.*

    I have already pointed out Mark 3:14, where the sequence is: be with Jesus first, then receive authority. So develop your relationship with God. Open yourself to Him. Receive from Him. But don't do so to get authority. Get close to Him because you love Him.

2.  *"Grow" for it.*

    Authority is given to those who are spiritually mature, not to novices. As we have already seen, the disciples followed Jesus for some time before He gave them authority. We shouldn't expect to receive a ton of authority the minute we start following Jesus. Growing in Christ means growing in faith and holiness. This is not to say you have to live a life of perfection to obtain authority. But if you aren't living a life of growing righteousness, don't presume to be graced with oodles of authority.

If you are struggling with a sin habit, authority is compromised; if you can't control that area of your life you have given place to the devil to control it. If we sin repeatedly, we give demonic forces legal right to influence or even control that aspect of our lives. If you don't have authority over your flesh, don't expect that you will have much authority over demons. Attempting to exercise authority over demons from a compromised spiritual life will actually be attempts to *control* demons. In other words: *Control is taken by those self-authorized. Authority is given to those self-controlled.*

> Control is taken by those self-authorized. Authority is given to those self-controlled.

3.  *Listen for the command, and obey it.*

As we have discussed, John 10 and Matthew 28 show that authority is communicated by an authoritative command. God has a command, mandate, calling, and assignment for each of us. When He tells us to go do it, He will provide the means to accomplish the task. Where does this command come from? First, it comes from the Word of God. The Bible is full of commands. Doing them is called *obedience* and ignoring them is called *disobedience*. When we do the things God has commanded us to do (not asked or suggested we do), we are beginning to walk in His authority. But if we deliberately ignore God's instructions, how do we expect to be able to function with authority in warfare? If we are not obedient, we are in agreement with Satan. If we agree with Satan, then we are obeying *his* command instead of *him* obeying *our* command—that is, the command of God through us. Revelation 2:26 says authority is given to the one who does the will of Jesus "to the end."

The second place we receive the command of the Lord comes from our spiritual leaders. Hebrews 13:17 says we must obey and submit to our leaders. Since the instruction to obey our leaders is in the Bible, then disobeying our leaders means we are disobeying God's word. Obedience to this instruction positions us in God's "chain of command." Disobedience breaks the chain of receiving and passing on authority. In Numbers 27:23, Moses commissioned Joshua to lead Israel. The Hebrew word for commission (*tsawah*) literally means "to command." Moses *commanded* Joshua to lead Israel. When God commissions, He commands. And when He commands, He provides the means to accomplish what He has commanded. There is authorization that accompanies the assignment given. And God authorizes people to pass on their God-given authority to some degree. God made Moses responsible for bringing the people to the Promised Land. Since Moses couldn't go himself, he gave Joshua the charge that God gave him.

From this example we learn that some of God's instructions to us will come from our leaders and mentors. They will give us assignments to help them accomplish the vision God has given them. When we serve our leaders and help them to accomplish their God-given tasks, they have the responsibility to serve us by launching us into *our* God-given assignments. Serve your leaders, do what they ask, and God will bless you and open up new opportunities for you. If your leader is a good one, he will encourage and bless you to pursue your God-given dream. If your leader is not working to develop you, or if your leader asks you to do something unbiblical or compromising, then ask God to change or exchange your leader.

A third place we hear the command of God is that personal call that God has for each of us. My mentor cannot take the place of the Holy Spirit in my life to give me a vision to pursue. Nor can I look up in my Bible's concordance for what career I should choose. But Galatians 5 tells me to walk in the Spirit. And as I am led by the Spirit of God, He will direct my steps. When we "hear" that leading in our hearts, we need to respond to it. This takes practice and faith.

We all have experienced missed opportunities to say a word for the Lord or serve in some way. Perhaps fear or insecurity got in the way. Whatever the case, the more responsive we are to the leading of the Spirit, the better we get at doing it. But if we continually ignore that voice, we are cutting ourselves off from the Spirit.

You may be in a place right now where you have cut off the leading of the Holy Spirit due to repeatedly ignoring the Spirit's prompting. Why not take a few moments right now to repent of that neglect and invite the Holy Spirit to once again speak to you and lead you. Then, decide today to put the past behind you and determine to step out in faith the next time you sense the Lord urging you. *When you feel the unction, it's time to function!*

4.  *Surrender to God; submit to your leadership.*

Before resisting the devil, James 4:7 says we must submit to God. The core of Christianity is "Thy will be done." Submitting to God is the first step in obtaining victory over the devil. When we talk about spiritual warfare, we usually think of our struggle with "principalities and powers." The idea of spiritual warfare evokes thoughts of confronting demons and rebuking the devil.

But there is another aspect of spiritual warfare that you might not have thought of. Besides the spiritual battle with the devil, every one of us faces another spiritual battle: the struggle of wills between what *we* want and what *God* wants for us. Jesus faced this battle in the Garden of Gethsemane. He asked the Father for a way out, because in His humanity

He didn't want to suffer. Twice He asked the Father if there wasn't some other way. Ultimately, He knew the whole reason He came was to die for our sins in our place, so He submitted Himself to the Father's will.

Jacob faced this struggle in a literal way. The night before he was to come face to face with his estranged brother, he wrestled with God in human form (Genesis 32). The result of that encounter was a new Jacob. He had a new name: Israel. As a result of the struggle, he got up the next morning walking with a limp, favoring the hip God had "touched." With every step he took, he was reminded of the wrestling match with God that changed his life.

Every one of us faces that spiritual battle with God. Our battle with the devil is a fight we must win. But our battle with God is a fight we must lose. We lose when we *surrender*. When we give in to God and pray, "Thy will be done," we are surrendering our will to God's will.

> Our battle with the devil is a fight we must win. Our struggle with God is a fight we must *surrender*.

"Losing" to God by surrendering to Him in this life guarantees our victory in the next life. And surrendering to God now is a prerequisite for defeating the devil. Surrendering to God doesn't make us losers; it makes us winners. Surrendering to God means we now fight a battle we can actually win—the battle against Satan. That's James 4:7. Submit to God, resist devil, and he (the devil) will flee from you.

In addition to surrendering to God, we must also be in submission to our leaders. This includes spiritual leaders (local church as well as denominational leaders), political leaders (even if they are on the other side of the party line; see 1 Peter 2:13-21 and Romans 13:1-2), employers, and family leaders (e.g., mom and dad). God has set up a certain order and we do well to comply with His order. True submission to our leaders is not based on their performance, because they will fail at some point. We submit not because of how great our leaders are, we submit because it is

> We must be *under* God's authority to have authority *over* the devil.

God's order of things. Submission is necessary to function in God-given authority. We must be *under* authority in order to *have* authority over the devil. When it comes to authority, *we must be under to be over.*

It's a scary thought for us to consider being under the authority of leaders who are inept, dysfunctional, or abusive. But 1 Peter 2 says to submit to *every* authority instituted among men. It says to submit not only to good leaders, but also those who are harsh (verse 18). In fact, Peter says our calling is that we should suffer under abusive leadership (verses 19-21), for in doing so we are following in Christ's steps.

Perhaps it would help if we had a proper understanding of what submission is. Submission is not groveling. It does not mean you stop thinking. It doesn't mean you will always agree with those over you. John Bevere points out that submission doesn't even *begin* until there is disagreement.[40] If you only submit when you agree, how do you know if you are really submissive? Submission doesn't necessarily mean agreement, and in some cases, it may not even mean obedience. If your employer told you to do something immoral, you can disagree and even be disobedient but still retain a submissive attitude. Of course, it may cost you your job. But then again, if you explain yourself in a humble, responsible way, you may impact him positively.

Submission is not some mindless, robotic subservience. Submission means *coming under another's protection.* A submissive wife is not one who follows her husband a pace and a half behind and is afraid to look him in the eye. We need to lose the Edith Bunker mentality of submission. A submissive wife is one who has come under the protection of her husband. That could be a scary thought, since her husband isn't perfect, can't protect her fully, and being human he will assuredly let her down from time to time. That's why submission and faith are inextricably linked. Submitting to any leader is an act of faith. We must trust God, that He will ultimately take care of us as we submit to His order of things. If we want God's authority, we have to be under His authority. And we cannot say we are submitted to God if we disobey His command to submit to all leaders He has put over us. Romans 13:2 says if we rebel against governing authorities, we are rebelling against God.[41]

In his book, *Pastors of Promise*, Jack Hayford points out that the Greek word for submission, *hupotasso*, means "to set in order." It's a military word assuring that the troops go out in a right order. They are ranked and structured in such a way that everybody knows how to protect one another so that no lives are lost and the enemy is defeated. The idea is that with this type of order everybody wins. It's not just the authority figure that wins because everyone is subservient to him. And it's not just that the subordinates win because the leader has to protect them. It's a healthy, mutual, win-win for everyone involved. It's entered into by choice, not compulsion, and God blesses both the humble submission of the subordinates and the humble service of the leader.

Speaking of the military, Matthew 8:5-13 tells the story of a Roman military officer who understood these concepts because of his military training. His servant was paralyzed and he went to Jesus to ask for help. Jesus immediately agreed to go and heal him, but the officer stopped Him from coming, since he didn't feel he deserved to have Jesus visit his house. Instead, he asked Jesus to just give the word, believing that Jesus' word would bring healing to his servant. He reasoned that Jesus was a man of authority, and he knew how authority worked because he was also a man of authority—military authority. In his military world, if he gave one of his soldiers an order, they had to do it because of the authority he had. However, if he didn't obey the commands of *his* superior officers, he would be stripped of his authority to lead his troops. With that understanding, he assumed the same principles would be true for spiritual concerns. Not only were his ideas accurate, Jesus found them amazing. He said, "I have not found anyone in Israel with such great faith" (verse 10).

This man understood authority. When he gave orders, he had Caesar (ultimately) backing him up. But he had to submit *to* Caesar's authority in order to *have* Caesar's authority. In the same way, when we surrender (submit) to God—let go of control—we position ourselves to receive God's authority. God cannot give us authority when we're hanging on to control.

Notice how Jesus' reaction to this man was that He marveled at his *faith*. Faith is necessary to be in submission. We have to trust (have faith in) God that He will care for us as we submit to imperfect leaders. Faith is also a requirement for authority. Remember, faith is not enough in spiritual warfare; we also need authority. However, without faith, you cannot have authority. Authority, as a gift from God, is received like any other gift—through faith. Faith gives you the confidence to step out and speak that word of authority. Belief alone without authority doesn't work; it's positive, but not powerful. Faith and authority work together to release the power of God.

5. *Ask someone with or in authority to pray for you.*

Earlier, we considered the "command" Moses gave Joshua when he commissioned him. This took place near the end of Moses' career and life when it was time to hand the baton over to Joshua. Here's what happened:

> [15]Moses said to the LORD, [16]"May the LORD, the God of the spirits of all mankind, appoint a man over this community [17]to go out and come

in before them, one who will lead them out and bring them in, so the LORD's people will not be like sheep without a shepherd. [18]So the LORD said to Moses, "Take Joshua, son of Nun, a man in whom is the spirit, and lay your hand on him. [19]Have him stand before Eleazar the priest and the entire assembly and commission him in their presence. [20]Give him some of your authority so the whole Israelite community will obey him....[22]Moses did as the Lord commanded him. He took Joshua and had him stand before Eleazar the priest and the whole assembly. [23]Then he laid his hands on him and commissioned him, as the LORD instructed through Moses.

Numbers 27:15-20, 22-23

In the posture of placing his hands on Joshua, Moses gave him "some" of his authority, as God had instructed. This was Joshua's *commissioning*. This transfer of authority culminated Joshua's training that took well over forty years. Jesus also mentored His disciples for a period of time before giving them authority. Remember that the first item on this list of how to receive authority is "get close to Jesus." Spending time in God's presence is a prerequisite to receiving authority, but so is spending time with a mentor and being taught by him. Jesus' disciples had the convenience of their mentor also being God in the flesh. We don't have that convenience! We need to spend time with Jesus, as the disciples did, but we also need training from our human mentors, just as the disciples received hands-on training from Jesus.

However, training alone is not enough, according to these examples. Training provides knowledge, skill, experience and character. The transfer of authority, however, is a spiritual activity that occurs with the laying-on of hands and, we can assume, an accompanying prayer for impartation. The apostle Paul also practiced this impartation. Timothy received a spiritual gift when Paul laid his hands on him (2 Timothy 1:6). Timothy was mentored by Paul in a relationship he described as a father-son connection (Philippians 2:22), yet the spiritual gift came through the laying-on of hands, not mentoring.

So choose your mentors carefully. It's not enough to have an intelligent teacher or a strong spiritual leader or a wise counselor. You need someone who can place his hands on you, call on Heaven, and be a conduit of God's power and authority in your life. And when a conduit touches you, you "con-du-it."

## Submit and Resist: The key to authority in spiritual warfare

Perhaps the most important verse in the Bible on spiritual warfare is James 4:7—"Submit yourselves, then, to God. Resist the devil, and he will flee from you." Many times, the only portion of this verse that gets quoted is "resist the devil," which leads to a misunderstanding of what James is teaching. Resisting the devil without first submitting to God is dangerous. We won't have God's backing and we cannot defeat the devil on our own strength or wisdom.

Some people think they are submitted to God, yet they still seem to get beat up by the devil. Why is that? There's a strong possibility they aren't as submitted to God as they think they are. Humble submission to the will of God is a powerful weapon against the enemy. Let me give you a dramatic illustration I once witnessed.

I had received a call one evening from a woman in our congregation. "How do you know when someone is demon-possessed?" she asked. I told her it's hard to say without meeting the person and listening to the voice of the Holy Spirit. She went on to describe a friend of her family's—a teenage girl I'll call "Christie"—whose behavior had become dangerously unpredictable. An otherwise stable individual, Christie would have episodes where she would throw herself on the floor and writhe and become violent. The things she would say were foul and abusive. When the episode passed, she resumed normal behavior. She had been admitted to a mental health facility, but they couldn't figure anything out and had done nothing for her.

Our youth pastor, Sam Snyder, and I agreed to meet with Christie and her mother. I'll never forget the look on her face when I first met her. Her eyes were daggers of hatred toward me. In the course of the conversation, she shared that unusual things were happening in her bedroom. Things would move around independently, and she would be awakened by a recurring nightmare of two demons. She had visited with a spiritist from a neighboring community and began to describe the demons to him. Halfway through her description, the spiritist interrupted her, accurately finished the description of the first demon, then went on to describe the second one, in detail, before she said anything about it! Apparently, these demons got around. He even knew their names. As we shared spiritual truth with her, I asked her to let us know about any unusual thoughts that might pop into her head. I explained that any demonic thought must be brought out into the light, exposed for what it was, and confronted. I encouraged her that those bizarre thoughts were not her own; she was under attack by them. As we talked, the thoughts did begin to come. She didn't want to share them at first, but eventually she did. "What are you hearing in your head?" I asked. She said to me, "I'm going

> Her eyes were daggers of hatred. "What are you hearing in your head?" I asked. She said to me, "I'm going to kill you."

to kill you." I reminded her that this was not her thought, but a demon's, and I wasn't impressed or intimidated by it.

So we explained how freedom works. We weren't going to do some Hollywood exorcism and be spiritual marines on her behalf. The ticket was this: Unless she gave her life to Jesus (i.e., *submitted to God*), we weren't going to attempt to take on these demons. If she didn't belong to Jesus, they had a right to be there. She wasn't interested, so the conversation ended, unresolved.

Then a couple weeks later her mother called me again. Christie was having episodes in high school. The high school counselor said—get this—"You either go back to those pastors, or you're going back to the psych ward." (That was a *public* high school!) So she thought it over, knowing she was trapped and that we wouldn't help unless she got her life right with God. So one night, alone in her room, she submitted her life to Jesus. Immediately, the episodes stopped. The nightmares stopped. The paranormal phenomena stopped. When she and her mother came in to meet with us a second time, she looked like a completely different person. There was a light in her eyes and she greeted us enthusiastically. We did pray for her that day, but it was more of a prayer of blessing than warfare. The battle had been won. By simply submitting to God, the demons had left without being specifically confronted.

But it doesn't always work that slick. There are stronger, more stubborn demons that won't give up so easy. About one particularly strong demon Jesus said, "This kind only comes out through fasting and prayer" (Mark 9:29). The devil must be resisted. Just as there are those who try to resist the devil without first submitting to God, there are also those who submit to God but don't resist the devil. It's another misappropriation of James 4:7, and it's committed by very sweet, sincere Christians who love Jesus with all their hearts. They are totally, completely, and sacrificially submitted to God. Their problem? They think that by having faith, praying for help, and trusting God, the devil will leave. As described above, many demons *will* leave on that basis, because they can't stand to be around people of faith who quote Scripture and trust God. It's not that it annoys them. It *terrifies* them. But some demons seem to be able to withstand more than others can.

For sincere Christians who don't take a stand and get in the devil's face with a bold word—"I bind you, spirit; in the Name of Jesus; I command you to leave"—they shouldn't be surprised if they continue to be harassed. When Jesus ministered to demonized people, He didn't play the role of "encourager." He didn't hold a Bible study. He didn't counsel them. He didn't even pray for them! Instead, He confronted the demon and ordered it to leave.

Why don't we do that? Some of us won't because we don't believe there are demons involved. We're Christian Sadducees. So we counsel and medicate people instead of setting them free. Or maybe it's fear that prevents us. *What if the demons don't leave? I'll look like an idiot. And if I rebuke them, it'll make them mad! That will make matters worse. Worse yet, they may jump on me and beat me up like the sons of Sceva!* That kind of thinking completely ignores faith and the authority that's available to us.

Another reason some Christians don't confront the enemy is because they're too nice. They are concerned that if we suggest someone is under demonic influence that we'll hurt his feelings. So we pray for him and encourage him, and that's all good and has its place and we could even stand more of it, but not when there's a demon involved. You offer a demonized person encouragement, and you may give opportunity for the demon to dig its heals in deeper because you're legitimizing the issue. "There, there. It's not as bad as you make it seem. You're really a wonderful person and God loves you." Sure, that's all true, but irrelevant right now. When the burglar is ransacking someone's house, that is *not* the time to tell him what a nice house he has. Tell him later, after you've thrown the burglar out or called the police.

Submit to God. Resist the devil. It's a powerful combination. It works. It works for everybody, not just certain, special people. The resistance ought to be done verbally, out loud, and with confidence. But you don't need to yell. Demons aren't deaf. Yelling is a misuse of authority. Ever known a mom that is always yelling at her kids and they ignore what she's saying? She has to yell louder and louder to get results, just like a drug that must be taken in increasing dosages to get the desired effect. Eventually, the kids tune her out. Why? They know she has no authority and she's simply trying to *control* them through threats, intimidation, anger, and decibels. But a child who knows that mom will follow through on her promise to spank needs only to hear mom's whisper and he obeys. Yelling at demons is usually an attempt to convince them (and ourselves) that we have the authority to do what we're yelling about. But if we have the authority, we need only confidently command them in the Name of Jesus to depart. They must obey. James 4:7 says so. If we believe the word of God is true, it shouldn't be a problem for us to believe this. That faith gives us confidence.

> Submit to God. Resist the devil. It's a powerful combination that works for everybody.

"Cathy" had that confidence and knew how to appropriately walk in Christ's authority. She had gone through our church's discipleship training and learned to apply it to her life in an extremely effective way. Her daughter, "Sheila," had experienced significant emotional wounds as a child and as a reaction to that pain had developed some negative thought-habits during her teenage years. She had a lot of death-thoughts and her low self-esteem became a dangerous emotional situation. She would often say and exhibit destructive things. On one such occasion, Sheila had made a negative comment about her life that was especially evil. Cathy had heard enough. She looked at her daughter and said, "I rebuke you, you spirit of death."

Her daughter, a Christian girl who despite what I have described was typically sweet and agreeable, answered her (or should I say Sheila's *lips* answered her), "By whose authority do you do that?" It was clearly not something her daughter would have normally said. In a normal situation, a child would respond with, "Excuse me? Are you talking to me? What spirit of death?" But a demonic presence, invading Sheila's lips, wanted to know what authority Cathy was operating under.

Cathy responded, "By the authority of the Name of Jesus and His blood." Sheila's lips responded, "Oh." And that was the end of Sheila's talk about death.

# CHAPTER NINE
# MAYBE NOW THE BIBLE WILL
# MAKE MORE SENSE

*T*he doctrine regarding Satan and the origin of evil I have been proposing might have been new to you before you began reading this book, but I don't think it's a new idea. I believe it has always been in the pages of the Bible, but we didn't see it because we didn't want to think about the possibility of God creating a being that was designed to be evil. We felt that raised too many unanswerable questions, and so we looked for an alternative belief.

The result was that we read *into* passages like Isaiah 14 and Ezekiel 28 instead of "reading out of" (the definition of exegesis) the texts. We read *into* the texts in an attempt to resolve the question of evil's origin. But in our attempt to answer the question of Satan's existence with the Lucifer story, we actually created *more* difficult questions. For example: How could Satan have turned evil while dwelling in God's holiness? And if Satan went bad while in heaven, can we also go bad once we're in heaven?[42] I think these questions demand answers if one adheres to the doctrine of "Lucifer's rebellion," and finding them in Scripture may be difficult.

Speaking of Scripture, there are many confusing Bible passages about evil spirits that really troubled me until I began to see demonic personalities as instruments in God's hand and part of His purpose in creating a pure bride. Let's look at several of them.

## 1 Samuel 16:14

This verse says, "An evil spirit from the Lord tormented" Saul. That's strange, isn't it? God Himself sends an evil (or "unclean") spirit to harass Saul. Why would God do that? First, the background of the story: Saul began his rule in an attitude of humility and obedience. He was so humble, he tried hiding in order to avoid being made king (1 Samuel 10:22). After they found him and made him king, he went back to plowing the fields rather than acting like a hotshot (1 Samuel 11:5).

But that all began to change when being king went to his head and he took matters into his own hands instead of relying on God. First, he offered a sacrifice that Samuel was supposed to offer. Samuel had told him to wait until he got there, but Saul and his troops were on the verge of battle and the troops were getting nervous. In offering the sacrifice, he tried to play the role of priest as well as king, and as a result Samuel told him his kingdom would not endure (1 Samuel 13:14). Then, Saul went to battle against the Amalekites, at God's direction, but he wasn't fully obedient (1 Samuel 15). Instead of destroying everything, he captured their king and kept the best sheep and cattle. His excuse was that he wanted to sacrifice them to God. Samuel's response was that *obedience* is better than *sacrifice*, because rebellion is the sin of witchcraft.

Because of Saul's disobedience, God was grieved that he made Saul king (1 Samuel 15:11) and declared that He would take the crown away from Saul and give it to one more worthy than he. Saul began to get suspicious that David was that one, so he tried to kill him a few times. By this time, Saul's behavior had become unstable and unpredictable. He was living for himself, disobedient to the word of the Lord, and so God sent an unclean spirit to torment him. In short, Saul got what he asked for. The demon was simply the consequences of his behavior. In chapter six I stated that two of the reasons for the existence of demons are to carry out God's wrath and to discipline disobedient saints. Depending on whether you believe Saul was a saint at this point, you can take your pick of one or both of these reasons that explain what God was up to. This foul, unclean spirit was actually serving God's purpose. And yet, in the presence of a worshiping shepherd boy, the unclean spirit left. It didn't like the soothing sounds of an honest heart worshiping God, so it would leave. It was demonic. It hated the things of God. Yet God sent it to Saul for a purpose.

## 2 Corinthians 12:7

In the New Testament, another Saul, renamed Paul, experienced the pressure of a demonic presence that God had allowed or even prompted. In 2 Corinthians 12:7 Paul described his "thorn in the flesh" as a messenger from Satan. What was this thorn? Some say it was an eye condition that rendered Paul nearly blind. This view is supported by verses like Galatians 4:15, which seems to suggest Paul had eye problems. Later on in Galatians 6:11, Paul signs his name with large letters, perhaps so he can read his own writing. Others, however, look at the context of 2 Corinthians 12 and suggest that Paul's thorn was the sufferings he had experienced for having preached the Gospel. Both of these views have merit.

I don't know whether we can figure out how Paul suffered from this thorn, but I think it's important to point out that the suffering itself was only the *manifestation* of the thorn, and not the thorn itself. The manifestation is not clearly defined in the text, but the thorn is. It was a messenger, literally an "angel," of Satan. Regardless of your position about the manifestation of Paul's thorn, we should all agree that a satanic angel is some type of demonic spirit. Paul had asked the Lord to take it away, but just like the demons that Jesus *didn't* send to the abyss or even force out of their region (their *assigned* region, perhaps?), God would not remove this demon from Paul's life. Three times Paul asked to have it removed and three times God said "no" because there was a purpose being served in that demon harassing Paul. One purpose this demon served was to teach Paul that God's grace was sufficient for him and that God's power is made perfect in human weakness (verse 9).

The other purpose this demon served was to keep Paul humble (verse 7). Paul had seen so many miracles, had done so much powerful teaching, and had so many incredible visions, that he could easily have become proud. But it's hard to be proud when you're suffering—suffering at the hands of a demon—especially when you regularly cast them out of other people! But once Paul realized the purpose behind his suffering, he began to delight (verse 10) in his difficulty. It's better to be humble and harassed than proud and victorious, because pride would have destroyed his ministry. "Pride goes before destruction, a haughty spirit before a fall" (Proverbs 16:18). This demonic nuisance, overseen by God's grace, was actually helpful to Paul in his ministry, and we benefit from it 2,000 years later.

## Judges 9:23

Back to the Old Testament. In Judges 9, God sent an evil spirit between Abimelech and the citizens of Shechem to achieve His judgment against Abimelech. This sounds similar to God using pagan kings like the king of Babylon to teach His people a lesson and to carry out His judgment. But in Judges 9:23, it's extremely plain that God Himself sent an evil spirit to do the job. That demon, created by God, served a purpose that's described in Psalm 109:6, "Appoint an evil man to oppose him." Why have a good person do the dirty work? Why not let the evil people destroy each other? Why not have demons do the destruction? That seems to be God's plan when carrying out judgment. Remember, "All things serve you," Psalm 119:91 says.

## 1 Kings 22:1-28

And now my personal favorite. The story told in 1 Kings 22 about the demise of King Ahab was always one of the most troubling stories in the Bible for me, until I learned that even demons serve a purpose in God's design. In this chapter, King Jehoshaphat of Judah paid Ahab a visit. Ahab invited Jehoshaphat and his army to accompany him in battle against Aram. Jehoshaphat agreed, saying they are like brothers and his army is Ahab's to command. "But first," Jehoshaphat suggested, "let's ask God about it."

So Ahab called in his prophets to give the word from God. There were 400 prophets who prophesied that day, each one declaring a great victory for Ahab. But something was fishy about these prophets. Even though they claimed to be prophesying in the Name of the Lord and speaking on God's behalf, Jehoshaphat could see that something wasn't right. So he asked Ahab, "Aren't there any prophets of the Lord around?" Apparently, Ahab knew these prophets weren't as legit as he pretended, so he confessed that there was one true prophet of the Lord he knew of, but he didn't like him because he never prophesied anything positive.

Ahab, incidentally, would have fit well in many of our American churches. American Christians have been largely seduced by teaching and preaching that promotes a feel-good experience. Teaching on repentance, discipline, fasting, and other "uncomfortable" topics are considered legalistic and not tolerated. Ahab would have agreed with that thinking. But gratefully, Jehoshaphat knew right from wrong and he chided Ahab, "You shouldn't say things like that." So the prophet Micaiah was brought to the kings.

The messenger who retrieved Micaiah advised him that all the king's prophets were prophesying a positive message about Ahab's victory, and if he knew what was good for him, he'd better do the same. Micaiah replied by saying it didn't work that way. He would prophesy what God gave him and nothing else. So when Micaiah arrived in the king's court, the king asked him if there would be victory, and Micaiah replied with an identical message that the false prophets had given. Somehow, Ahab knew that Micaiah wasn't being straight with him and he bellowed, "Micaiah, how many times do I need to tell you to only say what the Lord tells you to say?"

The Bible doesn't tell us how Ahab knew that Micaiah wasn't telling the truth. Maybe Micaiah made it obvious with his tone of voice. I imagine him with a cheesy look on his face and a sing-songy, sarcastic tone imitating the ridiculous false prophets. Whatever he did, he made it obvious that he was making sport of the false prophets. One of them eventually busted Micaiah on the chops toward the end of the story. After Ahab yelled at him, Micaiah straightened up and gave the king an answer to his question, but with more information than the king wanted.

First, he told Ahab that he saw Israel's army scattered because they had no shepherd. Ahab was about to launch into an

I-told-you-so speech to Jehoshaphat about Micaiah's negative ministry style, when Micaiah interrupted, saying he wasn't finished. He explained that he also got a glimpse into heaven, and he heard God ask the spirits surrounding the throne how He could entice Ahab to go into battle in order to be killed there. Different spirits had different ideas, but then the Bible tells us that a lying spirit stepped forward with an idea. His idea was that he would go among Ahab's prophets and spread an inspired message of victory. Except that it would all be a lie. God says (paraphrased), "That's a *great* idea! You will definitely succeed. Go ahead with your plan." Micaiah summed up his story by saying, "So you see, king, the Lord has determined to destroy you and He will do so through the lying spirit your prophets are quoting." It was at that point that Micaiah got punched. But that is exactly what happened. Ahab tried to prevent it by disguising himself as a soldier, but during the battle a random arrow struck home and he bled to death.

Let's think about what's going on here. There's a meeting in heaven, and among them is a lying spirit. Hebrews 6:18 says God cannot lie, so what was a lying spirit doing in heaven? Serving God's purpose by destroying a wicked king, that's what! This passage no longer troubles me, because now I understand that even the demons serve a purpose in God's design.

A footnote to this story: I believe that now, however, all lying, unclean, and foul spirits no longer have an audience with God because they were cast down when Jesus died on the cross, as described in Revelation 12:10 and discussed in chapter five.

### 1 Chronicles 21:1

"Satan rose up against Israel and incited David to take a census of Israel." The census was David's way of measuring how strong his army was. But because David was beginning to transfer the object of his trust from God to the strength of his army, God brought judgment on the nation. This verse makes it clear that Satan incited David to do this.

The same story is told in 2 Samuel 24. But in that version of the story, verse 1 reads, "Again, the anger of the LORD burned against Israel, and he incited David against them, saying, 'Go and take a census of Israel and Judah.'" Wow! That's pretty different! 1 Chronicles says *Satan* did the inciting. 2 Samuel says *God* did the inciting. David went along with it, and came under God's judgment for doing so. In the end, David repented and God punished, but He called off the worst of it. But what is with the two seemingly opposite views? How could one writer say God was behind it and the other Satan?

To understand it, we should know the Jewish mindset about the sovereignty of God. In Jewish thought, God was sovereign and in control of *everything*, so everything Satan did was subject to God's approval. So even when Satan did something, the Jewish view would attribute the act to God. To attribute it to Satan would suggest that God was not in control.

For example, we'd call a storm an "act of God," because God controls the weather, and we'd even get insurance to protect us from acts of God. (It raises the question about what other acts of God we insure against...) But the book of Job credits *Satan* with causing a storm that took the lives of his children (Job 1:12, 18-19). Jesus actually "rebuked" the wind and the waves (Mark 4:39). Why would He rebuke something God was behind?

The Jewish mind would have been cool with this. There was no contradiction. If Satan caused a storm, he could only do so with God's permission, so we could say either Satan or God did it. Our way of thinking can conceptualize these ideas, but we don't like it—especially when we try to hold the traditional view of Lucifer's rebellion. If we understand Satan to formerly be

Lucifer, the one-time beauty of heaven, the angelic-ambassador-of-God's-glory turned bad, then we will *really* struggle with these verses. With the traditional view, Satan's rebellion made him an enemy of God—an opposite, though weaker force that is trying to destroy God and His people. But if we understand that God created Satan as an adversary to test and challenge His people for their good, then we can understand the Jewish mind a lot easier. God *was* behind Satan's enticement, when we understand that God gave Satan permission to test David.

Remember, God cannot tempt anyone (James 1:13), but He does *test* them. However, the Greek word translated "tempt" in James 1:13 is the same word in Hebrews 11:17 where *God tested* Abraham (*peirazo*). You see, while Satan is tempting us, God is testing us, and

> While Satan is *tempting* us, God is *testing* us.

vice versa. It's two sides of the same coin. While God allows it, His desire is not that we will succumb to it, as David did, but that we will conquer it. When we defeat Satan's temptations (*peirazo*), we past God's tests (*peirazo*).

### Job 1 and 2

Reading the dialogue between God and Satan carefully, we might say that God picked a fight with Satan. God was the one who brought up Job and almost taunted Satan with how good Job was. Satan's response was like a kid saying, "Oh *yeah*?" Why did God allow, even provoke, Satan to afflict Job? Was it to prove a point to Satan? Hardly. That might have been a satisfying side effect, but God has Satan's ultimate doom sealed already, so it's a bit of a waste of time and energy to try to teach him what he already knows but hates.

So did God do all this so He would know what Job was made of? I don't think so. God, being omniscient, already knew what Job was made of. He knows the end from the beginning and knew how Job would respond and what would happen.[43] I believe that God did all this to prove to *Job* what Job was made of. In order to accomplish that, God employed Satan to bring trouble on Job. All the while Satan was attacking Job, stealing his stuff and killing his children, God was using all that difficulty for a greater, eternal purpose.

I can guarantee you that God has done, is doing, or will do the same for you.

# CHAPTER TEN
# A PERSPECTIVE OF VICTORY

*I want you to be wise about what
is good, and innocent about what
is evil. The God of peace will soon
crush Satan under your feet.*

—Romans 16:19-20

*A*s we near the end of this book on defeating the devil, we ought to stop and make sure we are keeping a proper perspective. My purpose in writing this is not just to correct what I believe are erroneous doctrines about Satan but also to explain why knowing the truth about the Liar is so important. However, while we're working on this we must not make the mistake of giving so much attention to understanding Satan's schemes that we get our eyes off Christ.

## First: Understand Who God is

If we are going to walk in freedom, we must first begin with a correct understanding about who *God* is. If we don't believe the truth about God we will not recognize His willingness or ability to rescue us from the spiritual, emotional, and physical trials we find ourselves in. If we don't believe the truth about God, then having an accurate view of Satan will be pointless, perhaps damaging. Freedom and victory begin with seeing *God* for who He truly is. For example, if we don't believe that God is a loving Father, we may conclude that our problems are insignificant to Him, so we won't ask for His help. Or, if we don't believe that His power is available to cure any area of bondage we might have, we may substitute prayer with excuses: "This is just the way I am; it's genetic," or whatever reason that drains us of our faith in God. The truth is that God loves us intensely. Isaiah 62:5 compares God's love for us like that of a groom's desire for his new bride. That's passionate love, not obligatory benevolence!

Psalm 62:11-12 says God is both powerful and loving. In other words, there is no problem that is so big that God's power cannot handle it, and there is no problem so small that His love doesn't notice it. He's a big God who notices small needs. He not only *has* the power to help you, He *wants* to help you! Like the leper who said to Jesus, "If you want to, you can make me clean," Jesus says to us, "I do want to…be clean" (Matthew 8:2-3, TEV). Failure to believe in God's willingness and ability to cleanse us will discourage or eliminate our prayers, short-circuiting God's work in our lives.

### Second: Understand who *You* are

In addition to needing a correct understanding about God in order to walk in freedom, we must also understand correctly who *we* are in relation to God. We will live up (or down) to the beliefs we have, and if we believe a lie about ourselves, we will live according to that lie.[44] If we don't understand who we are in relation to Jesus, we will struggle to walk in freedom even if we believe the truth about who God is. If we see ourselves as dirty, rotten sinners, we won't be surprised when we live as such, even if we acknowledge the truth of who God is. But if we see ourselves as redeemed saints, pure in God's eyes with a destiny to rule and reign with Him, we will begin to live up to that understanding. How we perceive our identity strongly influences our attitudes and behaviors. If we have a relationship with Almighty God, we have a new identity. My identity as "husband" is only possible because of my relationship to my wife. If I fail to be aware of the truth of my identity as Becky's husband, my behavior will not match her expectations, and my marriage experience will be a frustrating, not happy one.

A relationship with God is even more defining than a marriage relationship, because it is an eternal relationship with our Creator. A personal relationship with Jesus Christ redefines us. We have a new identity, as a "Christ-ian," bearing the Name of Christ. But what does it mean to have a "personal relationship" with Jesus? That can be a bit vague and can give people an incomplete or even false understanding of who they are in Christ if not defined and understood.

Borrowing again from the marriage analogy, there are a lot of husbands out there who are jerks. They made a commitment to their wives and, legally, they are married. But they don't act like they are married. In the same way, just because someone has a relationship with Jesus doesn't mean it's a good relationship. Consider this: Satan has a personal relationship with God, but it's not a very good personal relationship. In the first two chapters of Job, Satan appeared before God and talked with him face to face. Have you ever talked to God face to face? I haven't. Satan related to God personally—*very* personally—but not in a loving way.

A "relationship" with Jesus is not enough. It must be the right kind of relationship; a relationship that God has prescribed. Obtaining that type of personal relationship hinges on a correct understanding of God's nature and work. We must see Him as Father and relate to Him in a loving, submissive way. We must see Him as Savior and understand that the cross is the only means by which our sins can be forgiven and that His resurrection power from the Holy Spirit is the only means by which we can defeat the pattern of sin in our lives. But we must also see Him as Lord, which means daily obedience and spiritual discipline.

The Bible is full of descriptions and metaphors illustrating how we relate to God: He is Master (i.e., "owner"); we're His bride; He is the Comforter; we're His soldiers, and so on. But perhaps most significantly, we are His children, and unless we understand and believe that, we won't behave accordingly. Instead, we will continue to behave according to our previous identity: slaves to sin.

So the choice is ours. We can relate to God as Father, or relate to God as Judge. *Everyone* will stand before God and relate to Him personally, either as Father or Judge. A personal relationship is not enough. What *kind* of personal relationship we have is critical. So if we fail to understand and believe that we are God's children, we will struggle to walk in the freedom that a child of the King possesses. If we don't relate to God as Father, even if we have all of Satan's tricks figured out, we cannot walk in freedom. We will live according to what we believe.

## Third: Understand what You're up Against

In addition to a proper understanding of who God is and an accurate understanding of who we are in Christ, we also should know who Satan is. We should know what he tries to do and what our response should be. Just as every one of us will relate to God personally, for good or for ill, every one of us also relates to Satan personally, whether we are aware of it or not. Your relationship to Satan—how you respond to him—will have a significant role in determining your emotional and spiritual freedom. Just as we can choose to either relate to God as our Father or as our Judge, we can also choose how we will relate to Satan. We can relate to him as his *enemy* or as his *victim*. Satan is on the prowl looking for whom he can devour (1 Peter 5:8). Ignoring this Scripture doesn't stop him from doing so. If we pretend this verse doesn't exist, we are likely to be his victim.

Remember, this passage was a warning written to *Christians*, not unbelievers. If we follow the advice of that Scripture, to resist him, we relate to the devil as an enemy. So a proper understanding of God *and* Satan, and who we are in relation to them, is critical if we are to walk in truth and victory.

Let me illustrate. I played baseball in junior and senior high school. I was an average player on a good team. I was a better fielder than hitter, but I did OK at the plate. There was a pitcher from our main nemesis against whom I never got a hit throughout all my years of facing him. His teammates called him "Wally," a derivative of his last name. He had a decent curve ball but his strength was his fast ball. It didn't have a lot of movement but he had great control and he threw it hard.

In junior high, I remember him making me look silly on numerous occasions. He usually struck me out. I struggled to get the ball in play. In my senior year before our final game against his team, I told my coach, "I want Wally...*bad*." Because of the way the line-up was put together, I wasn't supposed to start. But my coach, seeing the fire in my eye, made sure I got a chance to pinch-hit against Wally. Wally put a big, fat fastball right where I like it and I went after it with everything I had... and hit a high pop-up to the second baseman. Six years and not one hit off Wally.

I share this story with you to describe the relationship I had with Wally. We were opponents. I'm sure he doesn't remember me, and even at the time he probably didn't even know my name. But I didn't care whether or not he knew my name, because it wasn't a loving relationship. It was a competitive relationship. Had my coach not known my name, that would have been painful. But my coach and I were in partnership, a different kind of relationship. A good one. But here I am, twenty-seven years later, and I still remember Wally. I remember his real name. I remember his bushy hair that stuck out from under his baseball cap. I remember, as a 98-pound eighth-grader, when Wally waved in the outfielders after seeing my slight form step into the batter's box. I remember how insulting that was and how I wanted to hit a screaming line drive past his right ear into center field.

My relationship with Wally illustrates the relationship we should have with Satan: competitors. (Not that Wally embodied evil, he just wore the wrong jersey!) Believe it or not, Satan is looking for a "personal relationship" with you. He is seeking relationship with you in which you are either a sympathizer or a slave or a victim. We should be none of those. Instead, we must be his enemy. That's a relationship; a relationship of enmity. Ignoring or neglecting that relationship does not make him go away. He won't ignore us. He's like a shadow that follows us. You can ignore your shadow, but it's still there. You can run from your shadow but it will follow you. But, when you face your shadow and chase it, it will flee before you. In the same way, James 4:7 says to submit to God, resist the devil, and *he will flee from you*. But who wants to spend their time chasing the devil? If we pursue anyone, it should be Jesus, and when we enter His presence and are surrounded by His light, shadows disappear.

As we have seen repeatedly, the Bible is very clear about the existence and presence of Satan in this world, and what we are supposed to do in response to his presence here. Failure to fight and resist him is disobedience to God's word. Ignoring Satan is not a Biblical option and leaves us vulnerable to his attack. And as we have discussed, if we are in a battle we should have some understanding about whom we're fighting and what strategies he uses, so we will be more knowledgeable in our fight. Not that this is our only strategy, but it's an important part. If we have a false understanding of our enemy, we will be less equipped to defeat him. For example, if we see Satan as equal in power to God, we will fear his attempts to destroy righteousness. Our fear will restrict our freedom and stifle faith in God. Or, if we see Satan as some unfortunate project of God's that went bad and had to be discarded to planet earth (the Lucifer-rebellion theory), we will fail to recognize the purpose his testing serves in our lives and may behave like victims instead of warriors.

However, if we recognize that God created Satan for a purpose, and that purpose is to...

...carry out God's wrath on sinners,

...discipline rebellious saints,

...strengthen and teach righteous saints,

...prove who is true and who is false,

...accent God's holiness, and

...provide humans a choice,[45]

then we will begin to behave accordingly. That is, we will be motivated to arm ourselves with the word, focus on Jesus, be filled with the Spirit, then resist and fight against the devil with the confidence that we will win.

When we understand that Satan was put into our lives for us to defeat, and when we believe that the word of God is absolutely true regarding how to defeat him, there's nothing that can stop us. Without that understanding, spiritual warfare can be a frustrating, uncertain nuisance. With a correct understanding, we can solemnly embrace the battle God has put before us—and win.

## To Summarize...

Without an accurate understanding of Who God is, it's impossible to walk in His freedom. Without an accurate understanding of who we are in Christ, our behaviors—influenced by faulty beliefs—will prevent us from walking in freedom. And without an accurate understanding of who Satan is, we will be uncertain about the authority we have over him. That understanding is helpful when we consider what spiritual warfare is supposed to accomplish: acquisition of freedom, victory, and healing, for the glory of God.

Emotional hurts are similar to getting a sliver in your finger. For healing to occur, the sliver must first be removed. Removal of the sliver in a spiritual sense is the removal or defeat of Satan's lies, accusations, temptations or attacks in our lives. It is spiritual warfare—a fight. We ought to understand what we're up against in order to have victory over that enemy. However, the goal of victory is not to kick demons around. We may need to expose, confront or even expel them, but the goal is restoration of God's people for the glory of God. Once the sliver is removed, we can begin to experience God's healing in our lives.

What does this knowledge and confidence look like in a practical sense? It means when confronting the enemy we can have confidence in knowing that he was put into our lives for a purpose, and that it is God's intent for us to win. So if we're walking in the Spirit and in submission to Jesus Christ, when we tell the enemy to "Go," he *must* leave. He has no authority. He was created to be defeated. He was put here to be overthrown by the cross and by those who have been cleansed by the blood that was shed on that cross.

> Satan was created to be defeated by those cleansed by Jesus' blood.

## So How, Exactly, do we Defeat the Devil?

There are many books in existence that provide instruction on how to do spiritual warfare. Rather than providing another how-to manual, my intent has been to *impart confidence* in spiritual warfare by looking at what God's word says about it. That confidence, a.k.a. "faith," is pretty helpful when battling Satan, regardless of your fighting style. So, my goal is to motivate more than instruct, so that you will be inspired to just get active in spiritual warfare. Remember, spiritual warfare is meant to be entered into by *all* Christians. So, if you are not in the battle, my hope is that you will be inspired and motivated to don the armor and start swinging your sword.

Though it is not my primary purpose to provide spiritual warfare methods, it would be perhaps unfair if I didn't offer at least a little advice on how to do it. I will close this chapter, and this book, by providing some warfare tips. In my opinion, James 4:7 is the first place to start, and the most important verse to understand, in order to be successful against Satan. The verse tells us to *submit to God* and *to resist the devil.* In chapter eight, we looked at "equipment" to arm and strengthen ourselves for spiritual warfare (the Word of God, prayer and fasting, faith, and authority). Those disciplines and tools are part of *submitting to God.* How does one go about the other part of spiritual warfare—*resisting the devil*? I leave you with a few weapons and offensive strategies against the enemy.

### Demolishing Strongholds

2 Corinthians 10:3-5 says,

> For though we live in the world, we do not wage war as the world does. The weapons we fight with are not the weapons of the world.

> On the contrary, they have divine power to
> demolish strongholds. We demolish arguments
> and every pretension that sets itself up against
> the knowledge of God, and we take captive
> every thought to make it obedient to Christ.

This is certainly strong wartime speech. We *wage war*. We use *weapons*. We *demolish strongholds*. We take "POWs" in the form of errant thoughts.

In chapter two, I defined what a stronghold is, borrowing from the insights of Francis Frangipane. He formed his definition on these verses from 2 Corinthians. A stronghold is a house made of thoughts, including arguments and pretentions, as verse 5 says. If you have demonic strongholds in your life, the battle needs to begin in your own life before doing battle with "powers" and "principalities" or even the footholds your fellow believer's battle. I'm not saying you have to be sinlessly perfect before you can pray with others for spiritual victories, but if there are significant strongholds or footholds in your life, you need to get free first. Matthew 10:8 says, "Freely you have received, freely give." You can't give away something you don't have. That would include spiritual and emotional freedom.

When the airline stewardess gives the safety talk on an airplane, she tells the passengers that if the cabin loses pressure a mask will drop in front of them. She advises them to affix the mask to their face before helping anyone else. Why is that? Because if someone fails in his attempt to help another, both will pass out. But if a would-be helper gets his own oxygen mask flowing first, he is equipped to share his "freedom" with all the people he can reach.

Ministry is similar. If the devil is draining your strength and joy by a secret sin or foul attitude, then you are not going to be effective in helping others step into freedom. Get yourself free.

Then help someone else get free.

Strongholds must go first. These strongholds, or destructive thought-patterns, form "ruts" in our minds that strongly influence or control our thoughts, emotions and behavior. Whether a stronghold is a demonic infestation, a thought-habit, undisciplined flesh, or a conditioned cerebral response is a matter for debate. Or maybe it depends on the situation. Perhaps they are all of these, or perhaps there are different types of strongholds. But if there are thoughts that are opposed to God's truth, the source and type of the stronghold don't really matter. Because if someone has built a house of carnal thought in his mind, he has "given a place to the devil" and is at risk for a demon spirit to take up residence in that area of his life, even if the stronghold began as simply a bad habit.

For example, the person who habitually doubts God's Word has built a mental house where not only a spirit of doubt can take up residence, but a spirit of fear, since not trusting God leaves him feeling afraid. That's why it's important to take thoughts captive, because sinful thoughts lead to sin. Clean up your thought life and you clean up your life. Let your thoughts run amuck, and sin results. Sin produces more sin and when you sin often enough the habit forms a habitation. Demons are attracted to sin and they need the agreement of sin to have the right to move in. Sin begins with a thought. That's why it's important to take disobedient thoughts captive by *surrounding them with the truth* of God's Word. That was the strategy Jesus used when Satan attempted to insert opposing thoughts into His mind. The three temptations were met with three Bible verses. Jesus knew the Bible well, as should we, if we hope to capture tempting thoughts with God's truth.

The place to begin demolishing strongholds is in the mind. Train your mind to meditate on godly things. "Whatever is true, whatever is noble, whatever is right, whatever is pure, whatever is lovely, whatever is admirable…think about such things" (Philippians 4:8). The easiest way to rid your mind of sinful thoughts is not to allow any room for them. Fill your mind with Scripture rather than trying to eradicate evil. If you remove the evil thoughts from an evil mind, what do you have? An empty head. But fill your mind with godly thoughts then the evil thoughts will be pushed out with no room to return.

The Psalmist said that the Lord was his stronghold (e.g., Psalm 27:1). Building godly strongholds with biblical thought is an effective war strategy to position yourself for the destruction of enemy strongholds. When the Lord is our stronghold, we have constructed a fortress with our thought life in which the Spirit of God can take up residence. Among these strongholds, like love and faith, is humility, possibly the most important stronghold with which to defeat the Enemy. There is simply nothing Satan can do with a Christian who does not succumb to pride, who has no interest in promoting himself and who consistently humbles himself before God and his fellow man. It doesn't give Satan anything to work with. Satan is always, always working at getting our attention off Jesus and on to ourselves. Even as we endeavor to remove demonic or fleshly strongholds in our lives, the devil's voice is present to get you to focus on your *own* righteousness instead of God's. Don't listen to him. Don't get into an argument with the devil about how righteous or how forgiven you are. Don't discuss your spiritual life with the devil! It's not his business.

The context of James 4:7 ("submit to God; resist the devil") says, "God opposes the proud but gives grace to the humble" (verse 6). If we cannot humble ourselves and admit we're wrong, God will oppose us. There are only two choices in this matter. We can submit to God and resist the devil, or we can oppose God and agree with the devil. Victory, deliverance, and freedom begin with humility. Admitting you're wrong and that your sins are ones Jesus died for is an act of humility that terrifies Satan. Fleeing, as James 4:7 says, implies fear.

Taking thoughts captive is a preventative strategy. But what about strongholds that already exist in our lives? How do we demolish those strongholds? 2 Corinthians 10 uses the aggressive, violent language of warfare, and that is what we will turn to now. The "weapons" we "wage war" with are not philosophies or advice that the world uses in its attempt to heal emotions and repair the mind. Rather, our weapons possess "divine power." Two of those weapons are described next.

## Addressing the Enemy

We submit ourselves to God with the words of our lips. Prayer is an act of submission and humility. Submission to God must include *speaking* to God, as in, "Jesus, I surrender to You." Resisting the devil is also done by speaking. Resisting the presence and influence of Satan and his demons is primarily done with words we speak *to demonic beings.* Speaking to the enemy may not be something you are comfortable with, but it is a Biblical practice. Jesus did it often, as did Paul (e.g., Mark 1:25, Acts 16:18). Resisting Satan means announcing to the enemy the will of God. Since the will of God is best represented by the Bible, it is incumbent for your spiritual health and victory to read, study, meditate, and memorize Scripture. Jesus resisted demons verbally. He told demons to be silent. He told them to leave. And he quoted the Bible to Satan. The Kingdom of God *advances* through words, especially the proclamation of the Gospel. Revelation 12:11 says Satan was overcome by the *word* of their testimony. Satan was defeated by words—the *message* of their testimony. The kingdom of darkness *retreats* in the face of godly words. Sometimes we need to, like Micah, speak to the enemy, "Do not gloat over me, my enemy! Though

I have fallen, I will rise. Though I sit in darkness, the LORD will be my light" (Micah 7:8). Quote Scripture to the Enemy. He doesn't like hearing it, so he's likely to leave you alone. When he does, that's called "victory." When he stays away, that's called "freedom."

Speaking to the enemy, however, is not something you should look for or enjoy doing. If you are seeking it, stop it. Instead, spend time in God's presence and in prayer and worship. Get your focus on Jesus. Forget about this book for awhile until you get your perspective back where it belongs. And if you enjoy talking to demons when you do deliverance ministry, then, friend, you are more of a diviner and sorcerer than you are a Christian. Conversing with spirits is for witches. We are not about chatting with demons for sport. That's sick. In fact, conversations with demons are not recommended at all. I can think of one time Jesus did it,[46] and that was the exception. Usually, He told them to be quiet. Some people get into deliverance ministry and they want to find out the demon's name, rank, and assignment, as if it were a POW. (Remember, we take *thoughts* captive, not demons!) Knowing a demon's personal information usually isn't necessary. And what makes us think a demon would answer our questions truthfully? John 8:44 in the NIV says that Satan's "native language" is lying. How can you tell if a demon is lying? If its lips are moving! So don't ask them anything, just tell them, as Jesus usually did, "Shut up and get out!"

Charles Mylander has appropriately observed that the Bible doesn't tell us with any precision how Satan organizes his kingdom. There are passages that give different names and titles to evil powers and maybe these Scriptures suggest rank, assignment or hierarchy. But we have to admit that the information is not crystal clear, despite the insistence of some people that they have Satan's kingdom reduced to an organizational chart and a roster. If we're honest about it, we ought to acknowledge that the Bible's discussions about the structure of the kingdom of darkness are a bit vague. Mylander says it's for a good reason. "If God told us precisely how Satan organized his troops, the tricky schemer would change it. Then the Bible would be full of errors. God is not stupid!"[47] Good point. So don't waste time trying to figure out what the Bible doesn't delineate, and what might be a moving target anyway. Knowing the Enemy's org chart isn't necessary to defeat him. Being able to tell him, "Leave," with faith and in the power of the Spirit, *is* necessary. He is defeated with words, not knowledge.

Warfare Prayer

I will leave you with one other weapon of spiritual warfare. And I end with this one in the hope that it will stay with you more than the previous weapon of confronting demons. This weapon of the spiritual battle is what I will call warfare prayer. These prayers are spoken to God regarding the enemy, but they are not the laid back prayers of sweet blessing that we typically pray. These prayers are intense struggles, partnering with God to overthrow the devil. Try commanding demons without first engaging in this type of prayer, and your results will not be guaranteed. Don't ask for your money back on this book if you command demons without success unless you first engage with God in strategizing, energizing, Spirit-led prayers of warfare. What does this type of prayer look like? The Bible provides dozens of examples. I recommend starting with the book of Psalms. More than just a song book, Psalms is also a book of war. The psalmists talk about their enemies in about one third of the Psalms. Usually, they are praying aggressively for the overthrow of enemies. For example, in Psalm 58:6, David prays regarding his enemies, "Break the teeth in their mouths, O God; tear out, O LORD, the fangs of the lions!" Why would

David pray to have their teeth broken out of their mouths? Because the mouth of the enemy is where the lies, taunts and accusations come from.

I believe it is appropriate for us to use prayers like these to silence the mouths of our spiritual enemies. For us, our enemies are not people, as they were with David. But the principles are the same. Jesus told us to love our enemies, meaning people. But for devilish enemies, we can adopt the attitude of Psalm 139:22, "I have nothing but hatred for them; I count them my enemies." Listed below are a number of warfare prayers from the Psalms that we can borrow today in our battle with the devil:

| | |
|---|---|
| Psalm 3:7 | "Arise, O LORD! Deliver me, O my God! Strike all my enemies on the jaw; break the teeth of the wicked." |
| Psalm 6:10 | "Turn back my enemy in sudden disgrace." |
| Psalm 7:6 | "Arise, O LORD, in your anger; rise up against the rage of my enemies." |
| Psalm 8:2 | "You have ordained praise because of your enemies, to silence the foe and the avenger." |
| Psalm 18:14 | "Lord, shoot Your arrows and scatter the enemies." |
| Psalm 18:17 | "Rescue me, Lord." |
| Psalm 31:15 | "Deliver me from my enemies and from those who pursue me." |
| Psalm 40:14 | "May all who seek to take my life be put to shame and confusion." |
| Psalm 60:11 | "Give us aid against the enemy." |
| Psalm 64:1 | "Protect my life from the threat of the enemy." |
| Psalm 69:23 | "May their eyes be darkened so they cannot see, and their backs be bent forever." |
| Psalm 69:24 | "Pour out your wrath on them; let your fierce anger overtake them." |
| Psalm 74:18 | "Remember how the enemy has mocked you, O LORD." |

| Psalm 74:23 | "Do not ignore the clamor of your adversaries." |
| Psalm 119:98 | "Your commands make me wiser than my enemies." Comment: We should pray for wisdom in warfare, but should also know God's commands. |
| Psalm 143:12 | "In your unfailing love, silence my enemies; destroy all my foes." |
| Psalm 144:6 | "Scatter the enemies." |
| Psalm 9:15 | "May my enemies fall into the pit they dug for me. May they be caught in the net they have hidden." |

There are more, but this list gives you a good start. The last item on the list is especially noteworthy. It's a good strategy for prayer in spiritual warfare. Psalm 57:6 says, "They spread a net for my feet—I was bowed down in distress. They dug a pit in my path—but they have fallen into it themselves." In chapter nine we talked about Ahab's prophets being inspired by a lying spirit. I believe it's a legitimate prayer of spiritual warfare to ask God to send deceiving, lying spirits into the enemy camp to cause confusion and disruption to the enemy's plans. Psalm 40:14 speaks of causing our enemies confusion, as does Psalm 35:26, "May all who gloat over my distress be put to shame and confusion."

*Prayers of Blessing instead of Cursing*

As we advance the Kingdom of light and push back the kingdom of darkness with words, the Enemy is also trying to expand his kingdom with words. And we are the targets. That's why 2 Corinthians 10 says we demolish "arguments." Satan uses the arguments of lies and accusations to promote his purpose. Believe those arguments, and his purposes advance.

Demolish them with Scripture, and his advances fail.

One particular form of word-weapon the Enemy uses is the curse. The idea of a curse usually evokes thoughts of witches and poisoned apples and other fairy tale stuff. Actually, curses are real and they aren't as mystical as you might think. Look up "curse" in your exhaustive concordance and you'll need the better part of an afternoon to look up everything the Bible has to say about curses.

Simply put, a curse is speaking evil to or against someone. Parents curse their children when they say they'll never amount to anything. Teachers curse their students when they call them stupid or lazy. There are also those curses uttered by Satanists, witches, and spiritists designed to invoke evil spirits to do their bidding. But most curses are uttered by the average guy on the street voicing a negative attitude. The power of those curses lies in the belief of the recipient. Tell a child he's an idiot, and if he believes it, he'll grow up thinking he's an idiot and he will probably act like an idiot. Tell a child she's worthless and it will stunt her self-esteem if she believes it. There doesn't need to be an evil spirit involved for that curse to have an effect. But if she rejects that insult and says, "No, I'm not worthless; I'm valuable," the curse has no permanent effect on her.

We can also curse ourselves. Have you ever made a mindless error and in frustration called yourself stupid? Maybe the mistake was, indeed, "stupid," but beating yourself up with insulting words does not help, nor does it glorify God. When you say things like that, you are actually coming into agreement with Satan and have merged your will with his, because he truly does think you are stupid. It's a word curse.

But God's word for you is that you "can do all things through him who strengthens" you (Philippians 4:13, ESV). So who are you going to agree with? Satan, who says you're an idiot, or God, who says you are more than a conqueror

(Romans 8:37)? This is not psychobabble positive thinking. It's what God's word says. If you do make a mistake, then repent, repair or recant, but recognize God restores. Jesus Christ paid for your sin already. Don't try to add to the payment with "verbal flagellation." Physical self-beating is what pagans do. When we verbally beat ourselves, we reduce our faith to pagan practices and Satan thrives on paganism. Instead of negative self-talk, we need to speak positively to ourselves, as Korah's sons did in Psalm 42 when they said, "Why are you downcast, O my soul…Put your hope in God." Or David in Psalm 103, who said to himself, "Praise the Lord, O my soul, and forget not his benefits." David speaks to his soul and reminds himself of several benefits God provides. David told himself, "Don't forget, David!" You might feel weird talking to yourself, but like someone once said, if you don't talk to yourself, your self will talk to you. And when we don't take those negative thoughts captive, most of us will naturally gravitate toward cursing, rather than blessing ourselves.

The curses we've discussed so far are the general, negative-statement curses of saying something evil to or about someone, including one's self. But there are, of course, curses that are uttered in the classical understanding by witches and other spiritists. Do they work? Actually, yes. Don't stick your head in the sand and pretend they don't.

In chapter seven, I introduced you to a witch I called Carl who attended our church for a season of time. I got some first-hand education on curses from him. He had moved to our community to live with a woman he had met on the internet. This woman had a daughter who was very disrespectful toward her mother. Her attitude irritated Carl so much that he stole one of the girl's rings and put a spell on it to make the girl behave better. Before he put it back with her belongings, he began attending our church.

One evening after he had attended our youth meeting, I noticed him pacing nervously in the foyer. I asked him what was wrong and he told me he was under great conviction because of the ring. I asked if that curse would really work. He said most definitely, based on his experience with spells. He described it as a strong spell that could not be undone. It was not the time to joke about bringing it to Mordor and throwing it into the fire of Mount Doom, but I did offer some ignorant suggestions. Could we pray over it? Anoint it with oil, maybe, and reverse the spell? No, he told me, it had to be destroyed. I told him if that was the only way, then do it. That night, he went home and pummeled the ring into oblivion with a hammer. Then he lay awake most of the night listening to the sound of knocking on his bedroom window. His *second floor* bedroom window. The knocking continued until we met with him and prayed for a breakthrough. Then it stopped.

Carl eventually fell back into witchcraft despite our attempts to persuade him otherwise. In fact, he got deeper into it than he had been before. One of the girls from our church happened to see him one day and struck up a conversation about what he was up to spiritually. He boasted that he could predict when people were going to die. Foolishly, this girl asked Carl when she was going to die. But Carl said, "Oh, I can't tell *you* when you're going to die because you're a Christian." How does that work? It works this way: A demon can no better tell the future than you or I can. But a demon has a bit more power to influence the future than we do. So when a demon "predicts" that such and such will happen at a certain time, there is an assignment sent forth in an attempt to order events to match the prediction.

I can predict that in ten minutes I'll get a glass of water. Not so amazing, since unless a meteor hits my home, I am in control of getting that glass of water. In the same way, the forces of darkness can predict when their "slaves" will die, because they have some control in killing them. But they have no right or access to children of the King.

What does this have to do with curses? The point is that the curse of a witch or Satanist has no power against a Christian who is walking in the Spirit. Proverbs 26:2 says, "Like a fluttering sparrow or a darting swallow, an underserved curse does not come to rest." Unless that Christian has compromised himself in some way and given the Enemy legal access to his life, those curses have no effect. In fact, a smart witch will know better than to curse a Christian, because it will have a boomerang effect. It will come back on him, as Psalm 7:15-16 and 9:13-15 imply.

We have seen this principle in action as well. My youngest daughter, Amber, is a gymnast. There was a new member on her team one year who was having trouble with her shoulder. We had seen God answer prayers for various injuries on the team earlier that year, so Amber asked the girl if she'd like prayer for her shoulder. The girl said no, saying that she had her "own gods." She had some New Age, animistic or neo-pagan type beliefs, so she began listing off the usual suspects of gods: the sun god and moon god and other such nature gods. Amber did her best to listen politely and respectfully, but when her teammate got to the "apple god," Amber blurted out, "*Apple god*?"

Her teammate said soberly, "Do not make fun of the gods or I will curse you."

Amber told her she wasn't making fun of the gods but added, "You just shouldn't make fun of the one, true God." When you say such things to such people you have just declared war.

So the girl went off by herself for a while and returned later to announce to Amber, "I have cursed you. You will always be sick and you won't be able to do the balance beam or vault well."

Amber came home and shared the story with us. So I shared

Proverbs 26:2 with her and we prayed for protection. The next day at practice, the girl sprained her wrist and, you guessed it, couldn't do the beam. The day after that, she had to go home sick. She tested positive for strep throat. Then she accused Amber of making her sick! And in the twisted logic of the enemy, Amber did sort of make her sick in the sense that the curse meant for her bounced back and returned to where it came from. But that shows how senseless the enemy's logic is, because we know that strep throat is a contagious bacterial infection, and unless Amber was a healthy carrier, she could not have possibly spread that infection to this girl. Fortunately, Amber was eventually able to make peace with this teammate and we even had her in our home for team parties. She was not a sorceress bent on ruling the world; she was just an overly-imaginative girl who needed Christ-centered spiritual direction.

All this talk about curses is to say that the kingdom of darkness tries to advance its work with words, and we need to respond with words—words of prayer and blessing. We can either advance the kingdom of light or the kingdom of darkness with the words we say. James 3:10 says we have the choice to either bless or curse. Proverbs 18:21 says the tongue has the power of life and death. And Romans 12:14 instructs us to bless and not curse. Words of blessing advance the kingdom of God and push back the kingdom of darkness. And Bible-based prayers are the most powerful, effective prayers you can pray. Don't think you can improve on what God has already provided. Make the Bible your strategy manual, especially the book of Psalms.

Another good book for spiritual warfare is Revelation. From what I have learned from others who have experience in spiritual warfare, demons don't like the book of Revelation. It is in Revelation 12 that we read about Satan being cast down from heaven, as discussed in chapter five. It's in Revelation

20:10 that we are told of Satan's future: a home in the lake of fire. Chapters 14 and 18 describe the fall of "Babylon," a reference to Satan's kingdom.

You say that you don't understand all the apocalyptic metaphors in Revelation? Join the club. You don't have to understand all of it to use it in spiritual warfare. Apparently, demons understand it fairly well and don't like hearing it, so use it. If you read the book of Revelation for what it is, instead of what we'd like it to be (where John is the Hal Lindsey of the first century), you will see the book to be more about *worship* than prophecy. In the first chapter, Jesus is *revealed* (hence the English name for the book) to John in such a dramatic way that he passed out (1:17). The description of Jesus in such majesty has to be at least an annoyance to demons, if not a source of overwhelming dread. The holiness and worthiness of God are announced throughout the book (e.g., 4:8, 5:9, and 15:4) and have inspired many songs you have probably sung in your church. It's a book of worship that exposes the defeat of the Enemy.

Sounds a bit like the book of Psalms where, in Psalm 8:2 we are told that praise *silences* the enemy. So the next time the Enemy starts bothering you, try saying something like this: "You foul spirit, if you don't shut up and leave me alone, I'm going to start reading the book of Revelation to you, out loud. So beat it!" It's just a thought.

### The Free Price of Freedom

So those are some of the things you can do in order to obtain victory in spiritual warfare and walk in freedom. But before we close this book and turn you loose to turn the world upside down, I must stress that it's not our efforts that defeat the Enemy, nor is it our faith; though we cannot hope to win without faith. It is the blood of Jesus that secures the victory.

Revelation 12:11 says they overcame the Enemy by the blood of the Lamb and the word of their testimony. There is nothing we can do to add to what Jesus did.

Shortly after the terrorist attacks of September 11, 2001, a man began attending our church out of fear. A lot of Americans returned to church, briefly, that fall, but many returned to life as normal after the initial shock had worn off. This man, whom I'll call Doug, had some very unusual spiritual beliefs. He mixed Christianity with astrology that sounded almost like Greek mythology. Those bizarre beliefs, coupled with the glazed, creepy look in his eyes, suggested to me that he was demonized. He came to church for several weeks, then quit.

A year or two later, we had special meetings with an evangelist who specializes in healing. I took that time as an opportunity to reconnect with people who had fallen away over the previous two years. So I mailed an invitation to Doug and was happy to see him show up at the first session of special meetings. It was evident that he was searching. He actually requested some one-on-one time to work through his beliefs. As I talked with him, I again sensed that there was a spirit of deception that had inspired his weird religious beliefs.

As we talked, he surprised me by asking if I would baptize him, though he had not committed his life to Jesus or shown any interest in what it meant to follow Him. I asked him why he wanted to be baptized. He explained that he had a "bad angel," and that if he got baptized that angel would somehow be cleansed and could return to heaven, freeing him of its presence. I told him I was fully aware of his "bad angel," but baptism was not the way to get rid of it. I explained what bad angels really are and how they attach themselves to us. I also told him that there is hope in Christ and that our church was equipped to help him get rid of his bad angel. He was relieved to hear that, then shocked me by asking, "How much does it cost?"

The Holy Spirit gave me a quick answer. "Actually, it's already been paid for. When Jesus paid for our sins on the cross, He paid the price necessary for us to be set free from sin and 'bad angels.'"

Like Doug, we need to recognize that disciplines like baptism, Bible-reading, prayer and fasting are all essential elements of building our faith and strengthening us for the battle. But it is not these disciplines that purchase freedom. They simply work in us God's ways so the freedom that was purchased by Jesus on the cross can be made available to us through the Holy Spirit.

Romans 16:20 says God will soon crush Satan under your feet. Have you ever heard of one of those revved up meetings where people literally stomped their feet and imagined they were stomping out the devil? I appreciate that zeal, though I question its effectiveness. The foot-stompers should be aware that it is not *our* feet, even in a metaphorical sense, that crush Satan. It's *God* who crushes Satan, but He does it *under our feet.*

Do you see the difference? When we "stomp our feet" on Satan, it's really God who is crushing him—under our feet. So we get to feel like we're helping, like a little child who "helps" his dad lift some heavy object. Junior really isn't helping. In fact, he may be hindering. But dad lets him push his little muscles against the object and he feels like he's Charles Atlas. But even as he strains those young muscles, he's getting stronger. So go ahead. Stomp those feet with all the little spiritual muscles you have. But stay humble and have faith in God, because He is the one who is doing the crushing.

And in your life, I pray that God would truly crush Satan completely…under your feet.

# ENDNOTES

## Chapter 2

[1] From the album, "For Him who has Ears to Hear," published by Sparrow Records, produced by Bill Maxwell and Keith Green, released May 20, 1977.

[2] The Bible uses the word *saint* to refer to any true follower of Jesus. We commonly use the word to refer to an exceptionally holy believer or something like that, but that wasn't the Biblical understanding of the word.

[3] *The Three Battlegrounds*, by Francis Frangipane, p.26.

[4] *The Three Battlegrounds*, by Francis Frangipane, p.29.

[5] As quoted by Leslie Brickman in *Preparing the 21st Century Church*.

## Chapter 3

[6] I would recommend Dr. Neil Anderson's book, *Victory over the Darkness*, for a discussion on the spirit, soul, and body.

[7] *The Three Battlegrounds*, by Francis Frangipane, p. 48.

## Chapter 4

[8] If the scholars that translate *heylel* as "shining one" are correct, then Isaiah 14:12 contains the only occurrence of *heylel* in the Old Testament. With only one example to work with, the interpretive process is difficult. There is nothing to compare it to.

[9] There are several examples of *yalal* ("howl") in the Old Testament. In Zechariah 11:2, *yalal* uses a form spelled the same as *heylel* in Isaiah 14:12. (A homonym. Remember that from English class?) But trying to fit "howl" into Isaiah 14:12 is difficult. Light-bearer or shining-one fits the context better.

[10] The Septuagint, abbreviated LXX, was translated in stages from the third to first centuries B.C.

[11] For the record, *Hesperus* was the Greek word for the evening star. It was apparently Pythagoras that figured out that Venus, the "evening star," and Lucifer, "the morning star," were one and the same.

[12] 2 Enoch is also known as *The Book of the Secrets of Enoch* and also as, *Slavonic Enoch.*

[13] *A History of Christian Thought,* Volume I, by Justo González p. 232.

[14] Someone—I don't remember who—once told me demons absolutely hate the book of Revelation. If that's true, it's probably because of verses like this one.

[15] González, p. 336.

[16] I am assuming there was not a pre-Adamic race. If there were people before Adam, it does not significantly alter my argument, though it might alter this particular point. Since the Bible does not clearly teach that there was a race of people before Adam, I am assuming that even if they did exist, they have little impact on forming essential doctrines.

[17] *Theological Wordbook of the Old Testament,* Harris, Archer and Waltke. Moody Press, 1980.

[18] The Greeks were the ones that started this myth about a god called Phaethon. There was a Canaanite version of this deity that the Babylon king would have been familiar with, as discussed by McKay, quoted in *Theological Wordbook of the Old Testament.*

[19] Ugaritic was a Semitic language of the city of Ugarit, Syria, with writings dating from the 14th through the 12th century BC. Ugarit was destroyed in 1175 BC, give or take. The Ugaritic language has been helpful for scholars in understanding Hebrew texts—specifically how common phrases, idioms, and expressions were used by surrounding pagan cultures.

[20] Daniel 5:30.

[21] New Bible Dictionary (NBD), p. 113.

[22] Although there is evidence that the temple of Bel existed until as late as AD 75 (NBD, p. 113).

[23] This "mount of God" is just that: a hill, not *Zaphon,* the mount of "the assembly of the gods" from Isaiah 14.

## Chapter 5

[24] Mark 6:31, Acts 14:28, 26:28, 29, James 4:14, 1 Peter 1:6, 5:10, Revelation 12:12, 17:10.

[25] *The Complete Biblical Library* Study Bible of 1 John.

[26] Jude apparently was quoting from "The Assumption of Moses," which is probably better named the "Testament of Moses." This book is

part of the pseudepigrapha and not accepted in the canon of Scripture. Apparently, there was a reference to this struggle described in the book, but part of the book was lost and this quote was apparently in the missing part. The early church fathers seemed to be familiar with it, but the quote has since been lost.

## Chapter 6

[27] The NIV's translation, "When he lies, he speaks his native language," is a bit of an interpretation.

[28] Jack Hayford sermon, *Why Sex Sins are Worse than Others*

[29] It is not the purpose of this book to solve or even address the issues of predestination, free will and God's sovereignty. When I say man has a free will, it is simply an observation of Scriptures that discuss the choices people must make. We can follow God and be blessed, or we can sin and be cursed. In Deuteronomy 33:19, Moses clearly admonished the Israelites to *choose* life. People debate over whether we actually have a choice or whether God moves us in the direction he has pre-ordained, and I also have my opinion on it. But this is not the place for that discussion. Whether we choose out of free will or choose out of predestination is an argument that will continue until Jesus returns—and maybe beyond (by those who were not predestined for salvation or did not choose to follow Christ!). Wherever the power and freedom of choice comes from, it's clear the Bible says we can choose between good and evil. Created in God's image, we share with God the ability to make choices.

[30] The Greek word is *tereo*.

[31] The Greek word is *hupakouo*

[32] *Theological Wordbook of the Old Testament*, Harris, Archer and Waltke. Moody Press, 1980.

## Chapter 7

[33] *The Complete Biblical Library* commentary on the Greek of Ephesians 6:12, p 169, Galatians – Philemon.

[34] Some translations, like The Contemporary English Version and Good News Bible make this clear: "all of you."

[35] Again, The Contemporary English Version helps make this more obvious: "Satan has demanded the right to test each one of you, as a farmer does when he separates wheat from the husks."

## Chapter 8

[36] I won't cite a page number to this idea, since it's repeated frequently throughout *Victory Over the Darkness* and *Bondage Breaker*. I cannot recommend these books to you enough.

[37] As quoted in *Preparing the 21ˢᵗ Century Church: Shattering the American Paradigm,* by Leslie Brickman.

[38] Much of the inspiration for this paragraph came from the "Faith Comes by Hearing" project.

[39] Neil Anderson, *Victory over the Darkness,* p. 113.

[40] Bevere discusses this in his books *The Bait of Satan* and *Under Cover.*

[41] For more on authority and submission, I recommend John Bevere's book, *Under Cover.* It is simply a must-read for every Christian.

## Chapter 9

[42] As I mentioned earlier, I am going to purposefully avoid the topic of God's sovereignty, predestination, "eternal security" and other controversial subjects, because it will get us off track. I'm already taking on enough controversy already! However, I can't resist posing just this one question related to this topic: Is it possible to adhere both to the doctrine of "eternal security" and to the "Lucifer rebellion"? would seem to me that one of the two would have to go. Either a person can forfeit his relationship to God (as Lucifer supposedly did when fell) or Satan was actually created as a vessel of wrath (as Roman describes) from the get-go and has always been a liar and murderer *the beginning* as Jesus said in John 8:44.

[43] Though I am avoiding taking a position on Calvinism Arminianism, I will take a position on Open Theism, a doctrine I I believe that God's sovereignty, foreknowledge and omniscience that even if He chooses not to control every aspect of history, He least see it coming.

## Chapter 10

[44] Neil Anderson, *Victory over the Darkness,* p. 47.

[45] This is discussed in detail in chapter 7.

[46] Mark 5:9.

[47] *Setting Your Church Free*, coauthored with Neil Anderson.

# Intermedia
# Publishing Group
## *Publishing That Works For You*

## Do you need a speaker?

ou want Russell Doebler to speak to your group or
? Then contact Larry Davis at: (623) 337-8710 or
ldavis@intermediapr.com or use the contact form
.intermediapr.com.

ou want to purchase bulk copies of *The Truth*
*Liar* or buy another book for a friend, get it
w.imprbooks.com.

book that you would like to publish, contact
Publisher, at Intermedia Publishing Group,
or email: twhalin@intermediapub.com or
rm at: www.intermediapub.com.

g
th
It
on
he
s 9
*rom*

*ersus*
*eject.*
mean
can at

p. 234.